YOUR ASSIGNMENT ☑ S0-BLT-594
A TERM PAPER OR REPORT.

—Have you been told what to write about—or
do you have to pick the subject?

—Are you in doubt about the proper elements
of a report or term paper?

—Is there any aspect of writing that worries
you? Sentence structure? Punctuation?
Vocabulary? Source material? Logical
organization? Your first outline or your
final draft?

If you are ever in any of the above predicaments,
this is the one guide that will clear up all your
questions and eliminate the time-consuming
process of trial and error. In it you will find all
the tools you need to take you in proper
sequence through every stage of writing a term
paper or a report—from start-up to finished
product.

# THE MENTOR GUIDE TO
# WRITING TERM PAPERS
# AND REPORTS

WILLIAM C. PAXSON is the author of *The Mentor
Guide to Punctuation and Spelling,* and three other
books on writing: *The Business Writing Handbook,
Principles of Style for the Business Writer,* and *Write
It Now!*

## SIGNET Reference Books (0451)

# The Mentor Guide to Writing Term Papers and Reports

## William C. Paxson

A MENTOR BOOK

**NEW AMERICAN LIBRARY**

NEW YORK AND SCARBOROUGH, ONTARIO

MENTOR TRADEMARK REG. U.S. PAT. OFF. AND FOREIGN COUNTRIES
REGISTERED TRADEMARK—MARCA REGISTRADA
HECHO EN CHICAGO, U.S.A.

SIGNET, SIGNET CLASSIC, MENTOR, ONYX, PLUME, MERIDIAN
and NAL BOOKS are published *in the United States* by
NAL PENGUIN INC., 1633 Broadway, New York, New York 10019,
*in Canada* by The New American Library of Canada Limited,
81 Mack Avenue, Scarborough, Ontario M1L 1M8

Library of Congress Catalog Card Number: 87–62620

First Printing, May, 1988

1   2   3   4   5   6   7   8   9

PRINTED IN THE UNITED STATES OF AMERICA

# CONTENTS

# ACKNOWLEDGMENTS

Debbie Hart prepared the graphics, for which I am most grateful.

I also thank two excellent teachers, Gary Christl and Michael Sharif. Gary provided almost all of the outline for the step-by-step guide described in chapter 1, and he and Mike donated their time to comment on other aspects of writing term papers. My use of their ideas and the ideas of others is, of course, my responsibility.

# PREFACE

This book is for students who write term papers. It is not a thin book. A thin book would not solve the many problems faced by writers of term papers.

If using a book this size seems to be a bother, think about this: The book you are holding in your hands is not intended to be read for pleasure. Instead, this is a reference book. Use it as you would use any other reference book, such as a dictionary or an encyclopedia. Dig into it from time to time to find answers to questions that arise while you are writing your paper. Use the book bit by bit, piece by piece—not all at one time.

W.C.P.

# INTRODUCTION

This book is for high school and college students who write term papers. A term paper is sometimes called a *research paper, research report,* or *report.* In this book the expressions used are *term paper* and *paper.*

Term papers are usually based on research. The research can take one or both of the following forms: (1) library research or (2) an analysis of materials presented in class.

The purpose of a term paper is to prove a certain point. The proof is arranged into three sections—an introduction, a main body, and an ending. The introduction says what subject the paper will deal with. Proof is presented and explained in the main body. The ending gives the writer's final thoughts on the subject. Other sections, such as a bibliography or list of source citations, also go into term papers.

To get the most out of this book, you should follow these steps:

- Skim the entire book before you use it the first time. Get some idea of the content of each chapter. Learn how to locate items of interest. Note that the front section contains a table of contents, and the back presents an index.

- Before writing any term paper, read chapter 1. That chapter gives you a step-by-step guide to writing your paper.
- While you are writing, treat the book as a reference book. Look up answers to questions that you have.

In addition, you should read the remainder of the introduction. It's a short, relatively painless lecture on two topics of vital interest. One is your reason for writing. The other concerns the chief character in anyone's writing—the reader.

As to why you are writing, the reasons are very practical. If you can perform thorough research and write well, you can get good grades in school. Moreover, the ability to write clearly is one of the keys to success in the world of work. In addition, society needs writers. We are flooded with information, either on paper or on a video screen. Somewhere, behind the scenes, people are researching and writing accounts of that information.

Other rewards can be named. Many people enjoy writing just as an activity. Many people enjoy library research, because a library is a vast storehouse of knowledge. In addition, a term paper can be an especially enjoyable assignment, because it is a chance to work on your own outside the classroom.

Moreover, your term paper is something that you yourself have created. You own it, and there's a lot to be said for pride of ownership.

While you are doing all the work of researching and writing the paper, think frequently about your reader.

Your instructor is your reader as well as being your teacher and your evaluator.

On one hand, instructors are some of the best readers to have. As readers, instructors make up a captive audience. They have to say, "I couldn't put it down" or "I read every word."

On the other hand, instructors are some of the toughest readers you will ever have to face. While reading your paper, your instructor is looking for weaknesses and mistakes. Your instructor wants to see how well you've done your research. Your instructor wants to see how well you can think through a subject and organize your thinking into written form. Your instructor wants to see how well you can use the English language.

To serve the reader, you must remember that the paper stands alone. That is, the writer is not there with the paper to explain or clarify points. The writing must help the reader understand everything that is in the paper.

Indeed, you have a lot of work to do.

# CHAPTER 1

## A STEP-BY-STEP GUIDE TO WRITING THE TERM PAPER

In this chapter you will find a step-by-step guide to planning, organizing, and writing a term paper. The guide will also help you narrow the subject to one on which you should not have to do an excess amount of work.

The steps are broken down into instructions and a sample assignment. Each set of instructions tells you what you should be doing at that point. The sample assignment is taken from a term paper submitted in a college-level course. By following the assignment, you can see how the instructions apply.

Although the instructions vary at each step, the assignment pertains to the same subject throughout the chapter.

### Step 1. Begin by Picking Three Subjects

Term-paper assignments take different forms. You may be given a specific subject to write on, or you may be given a list of specific subjects from which you may make a selection. In other instances you may be told to choose your own subject. In still other instances you may be given a broad subject and told to write on some narrow aspect of that subject.

When you are given a choice, begin by picking three subjects. If you start out with three subjects, you stand a better chance of having something to work on in case you cannot find research material for any one subject.

*Assignment.* Suppose that you are given an assignment that deals with impeaching a president of the United States. The assignment reads as follows: "Impeachment is a process by which a president may be placed on trial before Congress and removed from office. Andrew Johnson, our seventeenth president, was impeached, although not removed from office. In your paper write about some aspect of impeachment."

At this point you have not yet started researching the assignment. Like most people, you know something about impeachment and next to nothing about Andrew Johnson.

Therefore, what you should do at this point is re-read the assignment and look for key (important) words. In this assignment the key words are *Andrew Johnson, Congress, impeachment,* and *president.*

Those four words are four beginning subjects. You could settle for three, but with this assignment you have four.

## Step 2. Perform Preliminary Research

If the assignment requires that you use library sources for research, you begin your research by making the first of several trips to the library. You use the library to find at least three sources of information on each of your subjects. The sources may be articles, books, or chapters of books.

CROSS-REFERENCE: For help with finding your way around in a library, see section 2.1.

Some assignments require that you perform your research using materials assigned in class. These materials can consist of textbooks or assigned readings of articles, essays, books, or parts of books.

To perform your preliminary research using these materials, begin by checking tables of contents, indexes, chapter titles, and headings. Try to find at least three sources of information on each of your subjects. The source may be as small as a single paragraph or as large as a complete book.

*Assignment—continued.* This assignment is about the impeachment of Andrew Johnson, who was president from 1865 to 1869.

The subjects that you should be looking for are under the key words in the assignment: *Andrew Johnson, Congress, impeachment,* and *president.* You may not find one single book on the impeachment of Andrew Johnson. However, you should be able to find several books on the subject-key word combinations. The books may be available in the library, or they may have been assigned in class.

## Step 3. Find a Common Point in the Sources That Is Interesting to You

At this point you probably have a stack of books, perhaps a photocopy of an article or two, and maybe some notes. Now you need to begin zeroing in on a subject.

You do that by picking a common point in the sources that is interesting to you.

*Assignment—continued.* Different students would be interested in different aspects of the impeachment of Andrew Johnson. For our use here, let's assume that you are interested in what might have happened if the impeachment attempt had succeeded.

For certain, Johnson would have been removed from the presidency, and a new president would have moved into the White House. Your sources, however, describe other changes that might have come about. Congress might have become more powerful and the presidency less so. The role of the Supreme Court might have changed. Overall, the entire system of American government could have changed dramatically.

That these changes might have taken place sounds interesting to you. Therefore, you decide to research and write about this subject: how the American system could have changed if the impeachment attempt against Andrew Johnson had succeeded.

That is a subject. It is neither a thesis nor thesis statement. The development of those comes next.

## Step 4. Decide What You Want to Prove— to the Reader

A term paper is a *thesis*. The word *thesis* refers to an argument stated by the writer. The argument is for or against a subject. It is not that the subject is good or bad. Instead, the writer must argue a certain point of view concerning the subject of the paper. Moreover, the writer must prove that point of view, and the proof must be presented to the reader.

The argument is summed up in a *thesis statement*. A thesis statement is one sentence that says what the paper is all about. A thesis statement is the controlling idea, the guiding light of a term paper. Without a doubt, it is a good idea to write down a one-sentence thesis statement in your notes. Among professional writers there is an axiom that goes like this: "If you can't write your idea for a story in one sentence, you don't have an idea."

*Assignment—continued.* Based on preliminary research, you have probably convinced yourself that the American system of government would have changed if Congress had removed Andrew Johnson from the presidency. Now you have to decide that you want to prove those changes to the reader. Presenting the proof would prove your thesis.

First, however, you need a thesis statement, one sentence that will keep your research on the right track. To write a thesis statement for this assignment, begin by taking the subject that you had previously decided upon: how the American system of government could have changed if the impeachment attempt against Andrew Johnson had succeeded. Next, word it more strongly. Tell what the paper will show or prove.

You will have written something like this: "This paper will show how the American system of government could have changed if the impeachment attempt against Andrew Johnson had succeeded."

That is a tentative thesis. You might find reason to change it as you do more research.

## Step 5. Evaluate Sources to See If Your Thesis Will Stand Up

At this point you begin challenging the research material that you've collected so far. Your task is to question, question, question. Is the evidence there? Do you have facts to work with or just the assumptions and opinions of others? Do quotations from authorities support your thesis? Do you have much support or just a little? Will you need to get more? Is the support for your thesis easy to find? Is support for your thesis so obscure that it's a good chance your thesis is way out in left field?

CROSS-REFERENCE: For more help with evaluating research material, see section 2.2.

*Assignment—continued.* A tentative thesis statement reads, "This paper will show how the American system of government could have changed if the impeachment attempt against Andrew Johnson had succeeded." This thesis would be a difficult one to prove, for this reason: Because the impeachment attempt failed, no one knows for sure what the long-term results might have been.

Consequently, you would have to base your argument on material in two areas. One area consists of evidence made up of what actually happened at the time of impeachment. The second area consists of opinions of scholars who have studied this incident.

Concerning the evidence, a large body of research exists. It is factual evidence that shows how the American system of government did change during and immediately after the impeachment attempt. This short-term evidence provides one source of proof.

As for the opinions of scholars, they generally agree that a long-term change would have occurred. In your paper you could quote from or refer to the writings of these scholars.

## Step 6. Rewrite the Thesis Statement to Be More Specific

More than once you should challenge your thesis statement to see if it says what you want it to say. Remember, the thesis statement is the controlling idea of the paper. A vague thesis statement can lead to a vague, rambling paper and a lot more work than is necessary. On the other hand, a specific thesis statement can nail down a very narrow subject. A narrow subject can be developed into a good paper. Moreover, a specific thesis statement can save you from pursuing too many avenues of research.

***Assignment—continued.*** A tentative thesis statement reads, "This paper will show how the American system of government could have changed if the impeachment attempt against Andrew Johnson had succeeded."

One word in that thesis statement would present problems to any writer. The word is *how*. For this assignment you would have to put a lot of effort into showing how the changes came about. You would have to go into the mechanics of how the presidency and Congress work. You would have to *show* how impeachment changed the operations and relationships of the presidency and Congress.

A more narrow approach would be to describe *what* changes could have come about. Now you would not have to research and write up the *how* aspect. All you would be responsible for is the *what*. The change to your thesis statement would be minor: "This paper will show what changes could have occurred in the American system of government if the impeachment attempt against Andrew Johnson had succeeded."

## Step 7. Do Additional Research to Support Your Thesis

Now you do the bulk of your research and note-taking. Use your thesis statement as a guide. Ask question after question of your research material. Challenge each item of research to place it in one of these three categories: (1) support, (2) opposition, (3) trivia. Be thorough, yet brutal. You want many notes, but you cannot afford to waste time taking notes from material that does not apply to your paper.

*Assignment—continued.* The assignment concerns impeachment and changes in American government. The American system of government is based on a three-part division of power—president, Congress, and the Supreme Court. Research should be geared to answer questions such as these: What is impeachment? What kind of a man was Andrew Johnson? What kind of a president was he? Why did Congress bring charges against him? What is the background of the case? How was the case resolved? If impeachment had succeeded, what would have been the role of the presidency in the future? The role of Congress? The role of the Supreme Court? How would democracy have changed?

## Step 8. Develop an Outline

Develop an outline that is based upon three resources. One is your thesis statement, which you use as a guide for everything you put into the paper. A second resource consists of your notes. The third resource is made up of the questions you asked when you wrote your thesis statement and took your notes.

Your outline should cover points that you will write about in the introduction, the main body, and the ending. The outline may also mention the bibliography or other references cited at the end of the paper. Because the main body is the longest part of the paper, the main body should be the longest part of the outline.

To help keep readers interested, begin the main body with your most important point. To rebuild reader interest toward the end of the paper, place your second-most important point just before the ending. If you have trouble deciding what is important, remember that people like to read about other people. Featuring people in your writing helps keep readers interested.

Many instructors require that you use a traditional outline form. Other instructors prefer a sentence outline. Examples of both are shown with the assignment that follows.

If you are using a word processor, keep a written copy of your outline handy. An outline stored in a computer is not much help when you need it in a hurry.

And regardless of the type of outline used, remember that it is a plan, a guide. It is not necessarily the form that the final product must take. If you learn something during your research and writing that suggests a change for the better—by all means, make the change.

*Assignment—continued.* The first outline shown is the traditional outline. Topics and subtopics are arranged by roman and arabic numerals and capital and lowercase letters. If you use this outline, you should balance the parts; that is, if you have A, you should have B at least, and possibly C, D, or more. If you have 1, you should have 2, and so on.

```
Introduction

        A.  Thesis statement

        B.  Mention of participants

            1.  Andrew Johnson

            2.  Congress
```

I. Portrait of Andrew Johnson

    A. Description

        1. Appearance

        2. Education

        3. Character

    B. Johnson as president

        1. Early actions as president

        2. Plans for Reconstruction

II. The dispute

    A. Radical Republicans and Reconstruction

        1. Before the death of Lincoln

        2. After the death of Lincoln

    B. The Joint Committee on Reconstruction

        1. Committee members

        2. Committee actions

        3. A start toward impeachment

III. The trial

    A. The Articles of Impeachment

        1. Nature of the charges against
   Johnson

        2. Legality of the charges against
   Johnson

    B. Actions and reactions

        1. Use of political blackmail

        2. Actions in Congress

        3. Role of the Supreme Court

        4. Johnson's reactions

     5.   The vote for acquittal

     6.   Another attempt in Congress

     7.   Final acquittal

Conclusions

    A.   Changes in the system of checks and
        balances

     1.   A weakened presidency

     2.   A weakened Supreme Court

     3.   A more powerful Congress

    B.   Changes in the American system of
        government

     1.   A shift in power

     2.   A decline in leadership

     3.   Repercussions for democracy

Bibliography

Source Notes

Another popular outline is the sentence outline. A sentence outline consists of topic sentences (or questions) that describe points to be included in the paper. A sentence outline follows the form shown below. The order of the parts is the same as for the traditional outline, even though a complete sentence outline is not shown.

Introduction

    A.   Thesis statement:  This paper will show
        what changes could have occurred in the
        American system of government if the
        impeachment attempt against Andrew
        Johnson had succeeded.

    B.  Introduce Andrew Johnson and Congress as
        the principal participants.

 I.  Johnson seemed to be the ideal target for
     impeachment.

    A.  His appearance, education, and character
        alienated him from Congress.

    B.  His plans for Reconstruction were
        totally opposed to the plans of a
        handful of Congressmen. . . .

## Step 9. Check: Do Outline and Thesis Statement Work Together?

When you have completed your outline, check every part of it against your thesis statement. Every item on the outline must be related to the thesis statement. If not, you have to decide which one needs to be corrected.

*Assignment—continued.* If your outline and thesis statement work together, then move on. The next step in the process is the easiest and most relaxing.

## Step 10. Wait a Week

In the best of all possible worlds, you should have started work early enough so that now you can leave the term paper alone for a week. Give your mind a chance to develop new ideas or a different view of the assignment.

*Assignment—continued*. If you're well organized and ahead of schedule, let Andrew Johnson rest for a week. Like any other student, you have a lot of other things to do.

## Step 11. After a Week—Challenge the Thesis Statement Again

At this point challenge the thesis statement again. Make a determined effort to challenge it from the viewpoint of the reader. Your reader is your instructor, and your instructor will be looking for every possible fault.

To think like your instructor, ask yourself this question: What is it about the thesis statement or the thesis (the entire argument) that simply does not work?

Find that question and its answer. Write down the answer, but set it aside for now. You'll refer to it again in the introduction to the paper.

This is also a good time to come up with a title for your paper. The title should be specific, not cute or clever. To help clarify the title, you may use a subtitle. Both of these can be taken from the thesis statement.

*Assignment—continued*. Your thesis is that the system of American government would have changed if the impeachment attempt against Andrew Johnson had succeeded. Your proof comes from two sources. One source consists of quotations or findings attributed to scholars who have studied and written on the issue. The other source is evidence on the changes that occurred during and immediately after impeachment.

Neither source offers hard proof of what could happen in the future. The only way to get hard proof would be to see what happened if Johnson was removed from the presidency.

In the absence of hard proof, your reader has every right to ask, "Well, how do we know that these things really would have happened?"

The truth is, you don't know. No one does. It is a limitation of this paper. Still, you have to deal with the question; that is, you will have to deal with it before your instructor asks it.

You deal with a paper's limitations by explaining them in the introduction. In this case the problem could be handled with wording like "As scholars and the evidence indicate, these changes stood every chance of occurring, even though there is no way of knowing for certain." Set that sentence aside for use in the introduction, which is one of the last things that you will write.

As for a title, take one from the thesis statement: "This paper will show what changes could have occurred in the American system of government if the impeachment attempt against Andrew Johnson had succeeded." Possible titles and subtitles are:

How the Impeachment of Andrew Johnson Could Have Changed American Government

How the Impeachment of Andrew Johnson Could Have Changed Democracy

Impeachment of a President: How It Could Change the American System of Government

Impeachment of a President: How It Could Change
Democracy

## Step 12. Begin Writing—One Paragraph at a Time

Writing a paper one paragraph at a time is a conve-
nient way to work, because a paragraph is a small unit
of composition that is limited to a single topic. Some
writers go so far as to write one paragraph per page.
When the paragraphs are complete, they are placed in
order. The paper is then revised and completed.

When writing paragraphs you should plan them to
serve the reader. You can do this by (1) introducing
the paragraph with a topic sentence at the start; (2)
limiting a paragraph to sentences that describe, develop, explain, or support a single topic; and (3) presenting at least two sets of facts or concepts that aid
the reader in understanding the topic.

As you begin to string paragraphs together, you can
be alert for two of the biggest problems of term papers. One is the paper that meanders or rambles. The
other is the paper that is too short.

Rambling can be prevented by checking each statement in each paragraph. Each statement must fit into
its rightful spot in the outline, and each statement
must make a *solid* contribution to the thesis. Each
statement must *not* contain off-the-wall comments or
half-baked opinions.

If your paper is too short, then you haven't done
enough research. Go back to your sources for more

ideas, more quotations, more material to show that you have learned something about the subject.

*Assignment—continued.* The sample paragraph that follows is from a student paper on the impeachment of Andrew Johnson. The paragraph is limited to a single topic—the definition of impeachment. An introductory (topic) sentence offers a general statement about what impeachment is. Additional sentences present further explanation.

```
     Impeachment is not intended to be an inquest

of office by Congress but a judicial process

instead.  The rules for impeachment provide that

the House prepare formal charges and form a

committee to conduct the prosecution.  The trial

is to be conducted before the Senate and

presided over by the Chief Justice of the

Supreme Court.  A concurrence of two-thirds of

the Senators present is necessary for conviction.
```

## Step 13. Write the Ending

When you have written the paragraphs that make up the main body of the paper, write the ending. The ending may consist of several sentences or several paragraphs. Regardless of length, a well-written ending contains conclusions. Conclusions sum up what the paper was intended to prove to the reader. Conclusions are logical assumptions that are based on evidence presented in the paper. A well-written ending sticks to the subject and does not open up new avenues of thought. A well-written ending leaves no doubt that the paper has ended.

In addition, a well-written ending is not made up of minor details, apologies for inconsistent findings, or both. A well-written ending also is not a mechanical summary of content; that is, do not end by writing, "In this paper I have shown . . ." If you did a good job of writing the paper, the reader knows what you've shown. If your paper doesn't show anything well, the ending won't save you.

*Assignment—continued.* The following sample ends a paper on the impeachment of Andrew Johnson. Although the author does not highlight the paper's conclusions by using the word *conclusions,* the conclusions are there nevertheless: Democracy and the American system of government would have changed. The ending sticks to the subject and leaves no doubt that it is the final part of the paper.

It is easy to predict the outcome had impeachment been successful. The entire future of the legislative-executive relationship was at stake, for the removal of Johnson would have established the precedent necessary to make the executive branch a tool of Congress. The threat of impeachment would therefore hang over any president who displayed initiative or independence in administering his office. Congress would control the balance of power, even to the effect of reducing the authority of the Supreme Court. Such measures are of dubious constitutionality, but the Radical Republicans who pressed for impeachment had little regard for the Constitution.

An impotent presidency and a weakened Supreme Court: These are not what democracy has meant to the American people. Americans have revered their right to elect a president and have come to expect strong, dynamic leadership from the White House. This kind of leadership could not be expected from a president whose office was in jeopardy from day to day. Neither could this kind of leadership be expected from Congress, a large political body that is notoriously slow and bumbling in its actions. Worse, a weakened Supreme Court would be hard-pressed to serve in its primary role, that of being the ultimate defense for the individual.

It is hard to visualize a Congress that could control such an excess of power. If this were to be the outcome of the trial of Andrew Johnson, democracy as we now know it would not exist. In that case it could well be said that impeachment is the extreme medicine.

## Step 14. Write the Introduction

Before you start to write the introduction, think about this: How could you introduce someone to a roomful of strangers unless you first knew something about the person?

In other words, when you have just about completed your paper, write the introduction. Now you know enough about the subject so that you can do a good job of introducing it.

To write a good introduction, keep in mind what you *must* do, what you *should* do, and what you *should not* do. You *must* make clear what the subject of your paper is. You *must* state any limitations; limitations are the parts of the thesis that cannot be dealt with in the paper. You *should* try to capture the reader's attention by using a good first sentence. A good first sentence can be an exciting idea, quotation, or anecdote on the subject. You *should not* begin with a dictionary definition (Webster says . . . ), and you *should not* use the thesis statement word for word. Dictionary definitions and theses statements are dull.

If you're having a hard time writing the first sentences of your paper, try to incorporate these features: a key idea concerning the subject of the paper; some reference to a person or people; and some reference to time and place.

A key idea concerning the subject is important, because readers need to be reminded about the subject from time to time. True, they've seen the title, but a title is brief and a bare beginning. If at all possible, include a reference to people, because people like to read about people. A reference to time and place is also advisable, because readers like to know the setting.

***Assignment—continued.*** The introduction shown here is for the paper on the impeachment of Andrew Johnson. The introduction refers to a person (Johnson) and establishes the subject (change in the American system of government). Limitations (no way of knowing for certain) are given in the last sentence of the introduction. The thesis statement is not given word-for-word, yet the ideas present in the thesis statement also appear in the introduction.

```
     From the shadows of Abraham Lincoln's

assassination arose a dispute so severe that it

awarded Andrew Johnson the signal honor of being

the only president of the United States ever to

be impeached.  At stake was power--a more

powerful Congress and a less powerful presidency

and Supreme Court.  The dispute threatened to

change the system of American government.  As

scholars and the evidence indicate, the change

stood every chance of occurring, even though

there is no way of knowing for certain.
```

## Step 15. Complete the Paper

The list of steps given here is only a part of the effort needed to complete the paper. You will also have to pay attention to all the details of using words, punctuation, quotations, bibliographies, revising, and typing—subjects of the remaining chapters of this book.

# CHAPTER 2

# RESEARCH

This chapter lists library sources of information, shows how to evaluate information, and gives advice on taking notes. The chapter also advises you on the ethical and legal aspects of plagiarism and copyright.

## 2.1. Library Sources of Information

This section is a guide to research sources available in libraries.

**2.1.1. Beginning research: the encyclopedia.** An encyclopedia does not go into great depth on any single subject. Still, encyclopedias do give a little information about a great many subjects. For this reason an encyclopedia is an excellent starting point. Two encyclopedias often found in libraries are:

*Encyclopaedia Britannica.* Oldest, largest, and most famous of modern encyclopedias.
*Encyclopedia Americana.* One of the best general encyclopedias.

**2.1.2. Finding books.** A library's books are listed in its catalog. The catalog may be the traditional card catalog or a modern computerized one that relies on a video display.

In addition to searching the library catalog, you can try these sources when looking for a book on a subject:

*Books in Print.* Published annually; lists books still in print regardless of when published.

*Cumulative Book Index.* Published annually and serves as a record of books brought out for the year that the *Index* was published; books listed may or may not still be in print.

*Guide to Reference Books.* A standard listing of books in a number of fields.

**NOTE:** The term *in print* means that the book is available for purchase. Libraries shelve many books that are no longer *in print.*

**2.1.3. Finding articles.** If you want to see what articles are available on a subject, the place to look is a *periodical index.* Indexes such as those named here list journal, magazine, and newspaper articles.

*Business Index.* A microfilm reader that lists articles selected from more than 800 periodicals.

*Business Periodicals Index.* Covers more than 200 periodicals.

*Congressional Record Index.* The starting point to finding information in the *Congressional Record* itself, the latter a day-by-day record of activities in Congress.

*Education Index.* Indexes more than 300 periodicals as well as proceedings, yearbooks, bulletins, and monographs.

*Humanities Index.* Indexes more than 250 periodicals.

*Magazine Index.* A microfilm reader that covers more than 400 periodicals.

*National Newspaper Index.* A comprehensive index; a microfilm reader.

*New York Times Index.* Indexes the *New York Times* only.

*Reader's Guide to Periodical Literature.* Covers general and nontechnical periodicals; a longtime popular index.

*Social Sciences Index.* Indexes more than 250 periodicals.

*United Nations Documents Index.* A monthly list of documents published by the United Nations.

*Wall Street Journal Index.* Indexes the *Wall Street Journal* only.

**2.1.4. Finding out about people.** Brief biographies of famous people can be found in these sources:

*Biography Index.* A list of biographies found in periodicals, books, obituaries, and nonbiographical sources.

*Current Biography Yearbook.* Contains articles about living leaders in all fields of human accomplishment throughout the world.

*Webster's New Biographical Dictionary.* Contains more than 40,000 brief biographies of famous people, past and present.

*Who's Who.* The British counterpart of the American book (next entry).

*Who's Who in America.* A biographical dictionary

of notable living American men and women. Also published in these separate editions: *Who's Who in the East, Who's Who in the Midwest, Who's Who in the South and Southwest, Who's Who in the West,* and *Who's Who of American Women.*

**2.1.5. Finding out about places.** Information about places can be found in these publications:

*Hammond Medallion World Atlas.* Contains hundreds of political and topographic maps.

*Webster's New Geographical Dictionary.* Provides help with spelling, pronunciation, location, population, economy, and history of places identified by geographical, historical, or political features.

**2.1.6. Finding miscellaneous information.** An almanac is an excellent source of miscellaneous information. Almanacs are published every year. A standard work, which is well indexed, is the *World Almanac.* Also useful is the *New York Times Almanac.*

**2.1.7. Other library sources.** Libraries also contain specific reference works in many fields, including art, business, education, government, mathematics, sports, women's studies, and more.

**2.1.8. Other library services.** Other services that libraries offer include computerized research services, interlibrary loan, microfilm and microfiche, referral services to other libraries, and telephone research services.

**2.1.9. Other sources of information.** Research material can sometimes be obtained from sources other than school or public libraries. These other sources include newspaper archives, local historical societies, and libraries and archives operated by businesses, government bodies, and churches. Some of these are available to the public; some aren't. A telephone call will tell you.

## 2.2. Evaluating Sources of Information

Do not take sources of information for granted. The word *author* does not necessarily mean that the writer is an *authority* on the subject, even though the words have much in common.

You have to evaluate your sources of information, and you do that by challenging them. You challenge them by asking questions such as these:

**2.2.1. Is the publication useful?** Check a publication to see if it has a table of contents and an index. Glance at the headings, tables, and illustrations. Are they helpful? Read a few passages to see if the language is understandable. Is the publication theoretical or practical? Is it general or specific? Form some impression as to whether you should begin taking notes from it or put it back on the shelf.

**2.2.2. Is the source a primary source or a secondary source?** A primary source is an eyewitness account or an original document or manuscript. A secondary source is a work based on primary sources.

Examples of primary sources include the letters of Thomas Jefferson, the journals of an explorer, the

Constitution of the United States, and a participant's description of the Battle of the Bulge.

Examples of secondary sources include an analysis of the letters of Thomas Jefferson, a history book based on the journals of a famous explorer, an explanation of constitutional law, and an encyclopedia article on the Battle of the Bulge.

One source is not always better than the other. Personal memoirs and eyewitness accounts can contain errors of fact and are sometimes colored by the writer's emotions. The writers of secondary sources sometimes mention mistakes found in primary sources, but the writers of secondary sources can also inject opinions, biases, and conclusions into the account.

Overall, the best evaluation of sources relies on the use of both primary and secondary sources. Primary sources give the researcher the taste and feel of the real thing. Secondary sources provide insights as to the correctness and usefulness of primary ones.

**2.2.3. Does the writer cite sources?** If your source is a primary one, it is reporting original research or first-hand observations. Primary sources do not always cite other sources.

If your source is a secondary one, does it have a bibliography and footnotes? If not, does the author cite sources in the text?

Consider these words of William Manchester, award-winning author of biographies and other nonfiction: "I know that when I go into a bookstore and look at a book of nonfiction I look in the back to see if it isn't annotated, indexed, if there is a bibliography. Otherwise I'm not interested, because I don't know whether the fellow is telling me the truth or not."[1]

**2.2.4. Is the writer in his or her own field?** An expert on nuclear power has every right to criticize the educational system or, for that matter, anything else. Nevertheless, a degree in nuclear physics does not mean that its holder possesses the facts and intellectual basis necessary for writing on other subjects.

**2.2.5. What are the writer's biases and prejudices?** In the early 1980s this country was flooded with books about personal computers. The authors of these books had in common one characteristic: They liked computers. That was their bias, their prejudice.

If you had read those books without challenging them, you might have become convinced that the personal computer was the answer for everything from high-level calculus to a cure for the common cold.

Granted, computers do many things well, but there are many things they cannot do. The authors of those books omitted or submerged any aspect of computers that did not bolster their arguments.

It is the rare author who does not have biases or prejudices. If you do some tough-minded challenging of the writing, you'll uncover the flaws. Ask: Are the cards stacked in favor of something? Are opposing viewpoints considered? Does the author insult those who hold opposing views?

**2.2.6. Is the source based on fact?** Good writing is based on facts, and facts make up the foundation of any argument. A fact is a statement of objective reality. A fact can be verified by observation or judged reasonably likely because of evidence that is written down.

An aid to identifying facts is to classify them as *historical* or *scientific*.

A historical fact can be verified by records written by observers then living. Examples of historical facts include Napoleon's evacuation of Moscow in 1812; the San Francisco earthquake and fire of April 18 and 19, 1906; and the eruption of Mount St. Helens (Washington) on May 18, 1980.

A scientific fact can be rechecked at any time and its validity reestablished. Examples of scientific facts include the speed of light; the temperature at which water freezes; and the terminal velocity of a falling body in a vacuum.

Facts provide the evidence you need as part of research. If you don't see facts, you are reading assumptions or opinions. In the absence of facts, who's to say whether the assumptions or opinions are correct?

**2.2.7. Has the writer defined terms?** Suppose you read the phrase "neurotic adult attitudes." We are fairly certain what an "adult" is, and the word "attitude" doesn't pose any large problems. But what does "neurotic" mean?

Psychologists and psychiatrists use *neurotic* as a technical term, but casual speakers and writers use it to refer to any kind of personality problem that they don't like or want to make fun of. Consequently, if *neurotic* appears in a book written on a subject in the behavioral or medical sciences, the word might not require definition. Otherwise, if the word appears in a work meant for the general reader, a definition should be supplied.

Generally speaking, a writer should define terms that fall in two categories: (1) any term that might be new to readers and (2) any standard word or expression used in a new way.

**2.2.8. How recent is your source?** The newest book is not necessarily the best book. Nevertheless, new theories arise, and unknown historical documents are discovered. Do you have the latest word?

**2.2.9. Can you corroborate your information?** Suppose you interview the proprietor of a record store. He says that sales are down during the summer because students are gone on vacation. Don't stop there. Check with other record stores to learn if they have the same experience.

If at all possible, double-check your information by referring to at least one other source.

**2.2.10. What does the source tell or show?** Some sources *tell*; others *show*. A source that *tells* about poverty might simply say, "The poor lived in rundown apartments." A source that *shows* poverty would go into a lot of detail about how a rundown apartment looks and smells. The source would describe things such as dirty or broken windows, garbage left in the kitchen or hall, burned-out light bulbs, wallpaper torn and peeling, doors that won't close, plumbing that doesn't work, and on and on.

Generally speaking, if you are evaluating fiction you will have to be very alert to decide what the source shows. Writers of fiction devote a lot of effort to describing and showing, and it's up to the reader to pick out the message. In addition, some nonfiction includes quite a bit of descriptive detail. Again, the reader isn't told, but shown instead. Therefore, the task of evaluation requires careful attention.

You can ask some fundamental questions about the people involved: What do they look like? What kind of clothes do they wear? What are their emotions? What do they do? How do they act in a crisis? What does their speech say about them? What do they think?

You can ask about places and things: What do the settings look like? Are things old or new? What kind of cars do people drive? What season of the year is it? What time of day?

Remember the five senses: sight, sound, smell, taste, and touch. How does the writer appeal to each one of those?

And how does the writer *show* abstractions such as problems, conflicts, and goals?

Overall, always question your sources. Answers to questions such as those listed here are not in black and white and do not pose either-or situations. The questions are merely a means of evaluating a source so that you can judge whether to use it and how to use it.

## 2.3. How to Take Better Notes

Writers today have at their command three ways of taking notes:

- 3-by-5-inch cards. These cards fit into pocket or purse and are easily carried to class and the library. If you use many 3-by-5 cards, they become bulky. Larger cards are available.
- 8½-by-11-inch paper, three-hole punched. Binder-sized paper is easily transported and easily filed.
- The computer. Some writers keyboard their notes into a computer. That's okay, except for these disadvantages: Computers have been known to

lose material, and stored notes are not as visible as written notes spread out on a desk.

Whichever system you use, the following steps will guide you to writing better notes.

**2.3.1. Write notes in your own words.** Unless you are copying a passage that you want to use for a direct quotation, *write notes in your own words.* You do so for three reasons. One, you want the ultimate product to be yours, not someone else's. Two, the act of converting someone else's words to your own causes the words and the thought behind them to register more deeply on your mind. Three, you want to avoid plagiarism, which is the act, inadvertent or otherwise, of using as your own the words or thoughts of others.

**2.3.2. Copy quotations exactly.** When copying quotations, copy them exactly and put quotation marks around them as a reminder that what you've written down is a direct quote. Long quotations can be photocopied.

**2.3.3. Stick to the subject.** Writing tasks blend together. You will have to take some notes to come up with a thesis statement and an outline. At that time you may not have a firm grasp of what your subject is. Once you do, stick close to your outline and thesis statement when taking notes. Wandering down byways can be a waste of time and energy.

**2.3.4. Write on one side only.** Notes written on the backs of cards or paper tend to be overlooked, and it's a nuisance to keep flipping cards and paper over to check the back. Therefore, write on one side only.

**2.3.5. Keep notes separate.** Write one item per card. If you're writing notes on sheets of paper, leave space between notes.

**2.3.6. Identify notes by topics.** Identify each note with a key word that relates to the note's topic. Capitalize, underline, or highlight the key word in some way so that it is easily visible. Key words help you organize your notes. Each note should also show author, short title, and page number. A sample note card is shown in figure 2a.

Figure 2a
Sample Note Card

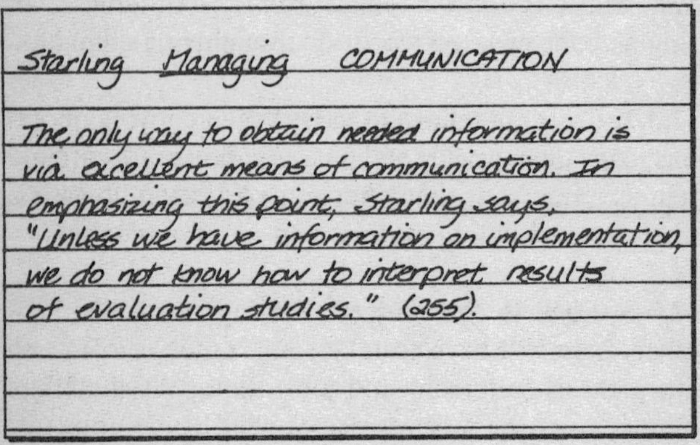

Starling Managing COMMUNICATION

The only way to obtain needed information is via excellent means of communication. In emphasizing this point, Starling says, "Unless we have information on implementation, we do not know how to interpret results of evaluation studies." (255).

**2.3.7. Make notes about sources.** For each source make up a bibliography card like the one shown in figure 2b. The card should show author, title, place of publication, name of publisher, date of publication, the number of the page from which the note was taken, and the library call number. Also include your evaluation of the source.

Figure 2b
Sample Bibliography Card

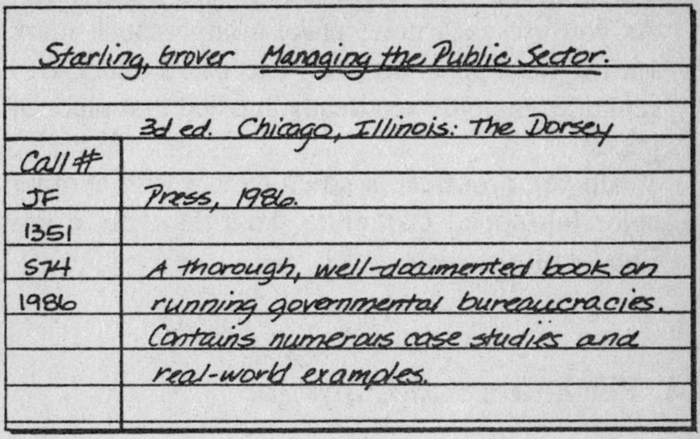

| Call # | |
|---|---|
| | *Starling, Grover  Managing the Public Sector.* |
| | 3d ed. Chicago, Illinois: The Dorsey |
| JF | Press, 1986. |
| 1351 | |
| 574 | A thorough, well-documented book on |
| 1986 | running governmental bureaucracies. |
| | Contains numerous case studies and |
| | real-world examples. |

**2.3.8. Record negative findings.** Write down any problems that you have with a note or a source. These problems might include a note that doesn't provide all the information you need or a note with which you disagree. Negative comments help you evaluate your sources and can save you the need of checking the source again.

**2.3.9. Be careful.** Write legibly, and write notes that make sense. Notes do not have to be grammatically correct, but you do have to be able to understand them. Be careful not to distort the meaning of what was said in the original. Get everything you need the first time through the book or article, and avoid return trips to the source. *And don't rely on memory!*

**2.3.10. Make the process visible.** You can incorporate notes into your writing by doing the following:

- Spread out notes, photocopies, and other research materials on your desk, on the floor, and on extra chairs. Make your research as visible as possible.
- As you use each note, make a large check mark with a felt-tipped marker. The check mark is a reminder that you've already handled that piece of paper.
- When you proofread a note, mark it with another color felt-tipped marker to show that you're finished with that note.

## 2.4. Plagiarism and Copyright

Plagiarism is stealing. It is the act of taking someone else's literary or artistic work and passing it off as one's own.

The penalties for plagiarizing are severe. Schools prohibit plagiarism, and a student who plagiarizes may be expelled. The plagiarist may also be sued. If the plagiarism violates copyright law, the plagiarist may be fined or imprisoned.

**2.4.1. Definition of plagiarism.** In its simplest form plagiarism is an exact copy. The writer who uses a passage word-for-word without crediting the source has plagiarized. Plagiarism also occurs when a writer uses someone else's graphic aid without naming the source of the aid.

Plagiarism can also consist of an obvious copy, even if not word-for-word. An example involved Alex Haley's *Roots,* a best-selling novel that won a National Book Award and a Pulitzer Prize.

Another author, Harold Courlander, charged that *Roots* contained passages from Courlander's novel *The African*. Courlander's book had appeared nine years before *Roots* was published.

According to Courlander, the similarities between *Roots* and *The African* included these passages:

From *The African*: " 'We are of different tribes,' Doume said. 'We bear different marks upon our skins. But as of today we are one village.' "

From *Roots*: "The voice of an elder rang out, 'Hear me! Though we are of different tribes and tongues, remember that we are the same people! We must be as one village.' "

Courlander said that "Certain scenes and dialogues, certain concepts and certain imagery in *Roots* do seem quite similar to various moments in *The African*."[2]

The similarities were enough to cause Courlander to sue Haley for plagiarism. During the trial Haley testified that three short passages in *Roots* had apparently come from Courlander's novel. As the six-week trial was drawing to a close, Haley acknowledged the plagiarism and agreed to an out-of-court settlement.[3]

**2.4.2. How not to plagiarize.** None of this is meant to frighten any writer from doing thorough research and taking many notes. After all, there are only so many concepts, themes, plots, characters, settings, episodes, and patterns. A truly original literary work is indeed a rare find, and two writers rarely do anything the same way.

Nevertheless, plagiarism does occur, whether on purpose or through carelessness. The best self-protection measures are:

- Write in your own words, beginning with your notes.
- If you use a quotation from someone else, place it in quotation marks and cite your source.

**2.4.3. Copyright.** As a student who is writing a term paper, you should also know about *copyright*. Copyright is the legal right that authors have to protect their work from being copied. In the United States this protection is provided by federal law (Section 101, Title 17, United States Code). The law does not prohibit copying altogether. Instead, the law provides guidelines on how much of someone else's work may be copied without obtaining permission.

Copyright law applies to your term paper if it is (1) published as an article or part of a book and (2) if it contains quotations, graphic aids, or other material created by another author. If in doubt, you can obtain information on copyright from the library and from the publisher of your paper.

# CHAPTER 3

## STYLE AND CLARITY

Style and clarity are dealt with in this chapter. The topics include agreement of subject and verb, gender-free writing, the objective style, the misuse of pronouns, sentence length and style, the use of transitions, the use of verbs, word choice, and word order.

### 3.1. Agreement of Subject and Verb

*Agreement* means to make nouns and verbs match in number; that is, singular nouns go with singular verbs, and plural nouns go with plural verbs. Two of the simplest examples are:

Singular: My *friend was* pleased.
Plural:   My *friends were* pleased.

The problem becomes complicated when several words appear between the noun and the verb.

*Each* (singular) of the students *is* (singular) going to graduate.

The word *none* sometimes causes problems in agreement. These problems can be avoided by thinking of *none* as meaning "not one":

> *None* (singular: "not one") of the students *is* (singular) going to graduate.

Another problem arises with a *compound subject*. A compound subject consists of two or more nouns joined by *and*. A plural verb form is used in a construction such as this:

> *A pen and a pencil* (compound subject) *are* (plural) necessary.

However, using *or* in place of *and* does not create a compound subject, and this sample is correct:

> A *pen* (singular) or a *pencil* (singular) *is* (singular) necessary.

Another form of compound plural is this one, in which the noun-verb agreement is wrong: "At one end of the main dining room is a fireplace and settees, comfortable chairs, and a coffee table." The simplest way to correct that sentence is to substitute *are* for *is*:

> At one end of the main dining room *are* a fireplace and settees, comfortable chairs, and a coffee table.

That sentence can be turned around and the compound plural brought to the front:

> *A fireplace and settees, comfortable chairs, and a coffee table* (compound subject) *occupy* (plural) one end of the main dining room.

The addition of an *s* at the end of a noun does not necessarily mean that the noun is plural. Each of the following samples is correctly written as singular, even though an *s* appears at the end of the noun in the subject. The trick is to realize that the noun stands for a singular item.

Economics is a hard subject.

General Motors is a large corporation.

Mathematics is an indispensable tool.

Ten thousand dollars is a lot of money.

An occasional noun without an *s* is correctly treated as plural:

People are fun to be with.

A dictionary is a good guide for showing whether a noun is singular or plural. Dictionaries show the following correct usages of three words that are frequently mismatched in issues of agreement.

| SINGULAR | PLURAL |
| --- | --- |
| criterion is | criteria are |
| datum is | data are |
| medium is | media are |

## 3.2. Gender-free Writing

The English language does not have a neuter pronoun for referring to people. The available pronouns are *he* or *she, him* or *her,* and *his* or *hers.*

Over the centuries, masculine pronouns have been used to refer to activities performed by men and women. As a consequence, the language gave the impression that life was for men only.

A more modern style, however, is *gender-free*. Gender-free writing works to treat men and women equally. The different styles, and their problems, are shown in these examples:

Each citizen must exercise his right to vote. (Not gender-free. It denies the fact that women vote.)

Each citizen must exercise his/her right to vote. (Gender-free, but the *his/her* combination is hard to say and read.)

Each citizen must exercise his or her right to vote. (Gender-free, but the *his or her* expression is a little awkward.)

Each citizen must exercise the right to vote. (Gender-free; gets around the pronoun problem by using *the*.)

One must exercise the right to vote. (Gender-free, but sounds too formal for some people.)

You must exercise your right to vote. (Gender-free, but sounds like a military order. In addition, second person—*you, your, yours*—is seldom if ever used in term papers.)

Citizens must exercise their voting rights. (Gender-free; gets around the problem by relying on plural forms.)

When you set out to write gender-free prose, keep these rules in mind:

1. Use combinations such as *he/she* or *his or her* as a last resort. Instead, use *one,* plural constructions, or *the.*

2. Don't mix singular and plural. Mixing singular and plural is ungrammatical. This sentence is a culprit: "Each *student* (singular) must be aware of *their* (plural) responsibilities." To correct it, write, "*Students* (plural) must be aware of *their* (plural) responsibilities."

3. Don't do anything far-out. When referring to a named character, don't use neuter forms. Joan of Arc was a *she,* not a *s/he.*

## 3.3. The Objective Style

A term paper is written in the *objective style.* The basis for the objective style is an *objective attitude.* To bring an objective attitude to your writing, you will have to set aside your biases, prejudices, likes, and dislikes concerning the subject of your paper. You will have to base everything in the paper on research.

When you write in the objective style, you as author stay out of the picture. Rarely is there any need to write in the first person; rarely is there any need to include *me, myself,* and *I.*

You do not have to write, "In my opinion, Johnson's stubbornness led to his downfall." You can delete "In my opinion" and use other wording, such as: "The evidence shows that Johnson's stubbornness led to his downfall"; "Johnson's stubbornness more than likely led to his downfall"; "Johnson's stubbornness apparently led to his downfall"; or, simply, "Johnson's stubbornness led to his downfall."

However, if you played a role in something described in the paper, that role may be worth writing about in the first person. If you do, prefer modesty over the ego-trip. You stand a good chance of alienating the instructor if you begin too many sentences with *I*'s or dot the pages with references to yourself.

In addition, remember these *don'ts*: Don't use the editorial *we* to stand for *I*; *we* is a plural word. Don't write in the second person using *you, your, yours,* or *yourself*. When you write in the second person you write *to* someone. A term paper is not written *to* the reader, but *for* the reader. Don't develop a so-called cute writing style. And don't write the way you talk—unless you talk in the objective style. Most people's speech is too informal to be converted directly to writing.

Finally, the job of a writer is to answer questions, not ask them. Therefore, most of your writing should consist of statements, not questions. That point is important, because you should not confuse a questioning attitude with a questioning style. Your attitude should be one of challenging your research and your use of words. Just don't let the questions show through.

## 3.4. Pronoun Reference

Careful usage requires writers to make a pronoun refer to its *antecedent*. An antecedent is the noun or noun phrase that appears immediately before the pronoun. Consider this example, in which the pronoun *it* is used carelessly:

The committee submitted its recommendation to the school district, but *it* took no action for six months.

Here *the school district* is the antecedent noun phrase, and the word *it* refers back to *the school district*. The sentence says the school district took no action for six months.

That's fine, if that's what the writer intended. Still, the reader has the right to ask, Was it the committee that took no action for six months?

If *the school district* is meant, say so, because the idea is to leave no doubt:

The committee submitted its recommendation to the school district, but the district took no action for six months.

If *committee* is meant, say that.

The committee submitted its recommendation to the district, but the committee took no action for six months.

If you don't like repetition, then rewrite the sentence:

The committee took no action for six months after submitting its report to the school district.

*or*

The committee submitted its report to the school district but took no action for six months.

The careless use of *this* (or *that*) can lead to confusion, as in these two sentences:

The safe driving campaign had little influence, cost a great deal of money, and used up large amounts of time. *This* leads to pessimism about any further campaigns.

Does *this* refer to the lack of influence, the cost, the time used up, or all three? What was probably meant was: "*These three* results lead to pessimism about any further campaigns."

Overall, you should use pronouns only when necessary, place them as close to their antecedents as possible, and take pains to make certain that relationships are clear. To make relationships clear, you will frequently have to repeat terms.

## 3.5. Sentence Length and Style

Most of your sentences should be short and simple, with a little variety thrown in from time to time.

**3.5.1. The need for short sentences.** Readers can take in only so much information at a time. At the end of a sentence, readers pause to piece together what they have just read. Short sentences enable readers to do this easily.

An example of what not to do is shown in the following sentence, which contains too many ideas for readers to absorb at one time:

> The forces that made mass society have suddenly been thrown into reverse, with nationalism in the high-technology context becoming regionalism instead, with the pressures of the melting pot being replaced by the new ethnicity, while the media, instead of creating a new mass culture, de-massified it, and in turn all these

developments paralleled the emerging diversity of energy forms and the advance beyond mass production.

A far better version is a paragraph of five sentences from Alvin Toffler's *The Third Wave*:

> The forces that made mass society have suddenly been thrown into reverse. Nationalism in the high-technology context becomes regionalism instead. The pressures of the melting pot are replaced by the new ethnicity. The media, instead of creating a mass culture, de-massify it. In turn, all these developments parallel the merging diversity of energy forms and the advance beyond mass production.[1]

**3.5.2. The need for simplicity.** Sentences become hard to follow when they are crammed full of information. This problem can arise when the writer overloads the sentence with parenthetical ideas or other internal elements that interrupt the flow of information.

If that is the case, the interrupting ideas can be removed and placed in a separate sentence or separate sentences. This sentence can be simplified:

> Nations in an expansionist mood—where time becomes important and where haste and energy (visible activity) and practicality prevail—are places where spare time is hard to find.

That sentence is adapted from Sebastian de Grazia's *Of Time, Work, and Leisure*. De Grazia's version consisted of three sentences that packed some punch:

> Nations in an expansionist mood are places where spare time is hard to find. Time becomes important. Haste and energy (visible activity) and practicality prevail.[2]

**3.5.3. The need for variety.** Not all sentences should be simple, and not all sentences should be short. Variety helps to keep readers awake. An excellent example of variations in sentence length and style is this paragraph from Vance Packard's *The People Shapers*.

> The announcement by Bevis came as quite a shock to scientists in several countries who had been working on test-tube fertilization and embryo transfer. Bevis had not been counted among the front runners, although it was known that he had been working in the field. Two of his countrymen—R. G. Edwards, a physiologist at Cambridge University, and his working partner, Patrick Steptoe, an obstetrician at Oldham General Hospital—were far better known. They had massive funding. They had worked with hundreds of women volunteers. And their efforts had received wide attention. Steptoe made a critical and skeptical statement when Bevis announced his feat.[3]

Overall, the majority of your sentences should be short and simple. Then throw in enough variety to jolt readers from time to time.

## 3.6. Transitional Words and Phrases

A transition may be a word or a phrase. You use transitions to link one idea to the next and to smooth out the reading.

A frequent use of transitions is to link sentences within a paragraph. In the following paragraph, the words *instead* and *therefore* are transitions:

> Inventive, group-experience teaching methods may not work in a staid college course that is required of all

freshmen. *Instead*, what is needed is a learning environment that will forestall the development of apathetic, bitter, or negative attitudes among students. *Therefore*, what is needed is a teaching method that makes the dull course become inviting and productive.

A transition can also join one paragraph to the next. In this next example, the word *nevertheless* helps connect two paragraphs:

> The plot dealt with the assassination of Julius Caesar by Brutus and his co-conspirators, and with the successful revenge of Antony and Octavius for the murderous deed. In that respect, the movie was like the play.
>
> *Nevertheless*, the movie failed to explain why it was necessary to destroy Caesar . . .

Transitions improve *continuity*. Continuity is the flow of ideas. Transitions also improve *coherence*. Coherence is how well ideas stick together.

Another way of improving continuity and coherence is to repeat words and ideas, as in this next example. Here the repeated words are *thesis* and *acceptance*:

> Merton's *thesis* at first drew only polite *acceptance*. In a few short years, however, his *thesis* came to be recognized as possessing a large degree of truth, and *acceptance* widened. Today the Merton *thesis* is accepted as a universal fact, although few people have ever heard of the name Merton.

Some sample transitional words and phrases are:

TO INTRODUCE A TOPIC

| | |
|---|---|
| additionally | furthermore |
| and | in addition |
| another | moreover |
| a second point | similarly |

TO RESTATE A POINT

in other words
that is to say
to put it differently

TO CONCEDE A POINT

granted
of course
to be sure

AS PART OF CAUSE AND EFFECT

| | |
|---|---|
| accordingly | consequently |
| as a result | therefore |

TO POINT THE READER IN THE RIGHT DIRECTION

| | |
|---|---|
| across the continent | there |
| here | in the southern part of the state |

TO GUIDE THE READER THROUGH TIME

| | |
|---|---|
| after several weeks | later |
| during all this time | next |
| earlier | then |
| for the first time | ultimately |

TO CONCLUDE

| | |
|---|---|
| all in all | in conclusion |
| finally | to summarize |

CROSS-REFERENCE: Punctuation with transitions is the subject of section 5.1.2.

## 3.7. Verbs

Verbs are the action words of language. Verbs are the *do* words. Verbs put movement and vigor into prose. The skillful use of verbs can go a long way toward making the dullest subject readable. Verbs deserve all the attention you can give them.

**3.7.1. Active versus passive voice.** *Voice* is a term used to show how a sentence is arranged around its verb or verb phrase. Voice can be *active* or *passive*.

In active voice the underlying logic is who did what to whom. In active voice the emphasis is on the doer of the action, the agent, the acting force.

When passive voice is used, the who-does-what order is reversed. The focus of the sentence shifts to emphasize the object of the action.

In the examples that follow, the DOER OF THE ACTION IS CAPITALIZED, *the verb or verb phrase is italicized,* and the object of the action is lowercased.

Active: THE SOLDIERS *played* baseball between battles.
Passive: Baseball *was played* by THE SOLDIERS between battles.
Active: CHIANG KAI-SHEK *knew* almost nothing of conditions in his domain.
Passive: Almost nothing of conditions in his domain *was known* by CHIANG KAI-SHEK.

Notice what happens when the same subject is written about in active or passive voice. The active voice form is shorter, more to the point, and follows the who-does-what sequence. In passive voice, the sentences become longer and more confusing; they become confusing because readers do not readily see the who-does-what sequence.

In short, the majority of your writing should be in active voice, because active voice helps lead to strong, vigorous prose.

Still, passive voice has its uses. If the doer of the action is not important, then use passive voice to move the important idea to the front of the sentence. If a dog bites the president of the United States, people want to know first about the president, then the dog:

> The president *was bitten* by A DOG.

The passive voice may also be used when the performer of the action is not known or important:

> Some of his brain cells *were damaged* when he was a child.

**3.7.2.** *It is, there is, there are* **constructions.** Nothing is wrong with using an occasional *it is, there is,* or *there are* construction. Still, the frequent use of those verb forms is monotonous to read. Rewriting them is usually easy. As an example:

> It was a hot morning early in September when school opened.

That sentence becomes a lot stronger by dropping *It was* and moving the verb *opened* to a more prominent spot near the front of the sentence:

> School opened on a hot morning early in September.

**3.7.3. Historical present.** The *historical present* uses verbs in the present tense to refer to past events.

Writers of literary critiques often use the historical present even though the author they are writing about is dead.

Therefore, you see expressions like "Harrison writes" when Harrison is no longer writing and has long since departed the earthly vale.

The use of the historical present is acceptable even though it sounds odd to many readers. Past tense will work quite well, and to say "Harrison wrote" is also acceptable.

Whatever you do, be consistent. If you begin describing a literary work by using the historical present, stick with it. If you favor the past tense, stick with that.

**3.7.4. Order of tenses.** People who write about historical subjects sometimes have difficulty in selecting the right verb tense. Part of that difficulty can be traced to the traditional names of the tenses, which are:

present     present perfect     past     past perfect

For the purposes of working out the tenses here, however, the following names apply.

present     connecting     past     past past

The present tense is used to report on an event that is happening now:

Johnson *works* hard.

The present tense is also used to describe a universal truth, such as:

The earth *revolves* around the sun.

The connecting (present perfect) tense is used to describe an action that started in the past and is continuing in or connected to the present:

> Because Johnson *has worked* so hard on her assignment, she should get a good grade. (Johnson may still be working on her assignment, or it may not yet be graded. Either way, the event is still continuing.)

The past tense is used to describe past actions that are linked to a definite time or set of conditions:

> Johnson *worked* hard on her assignment last week.

The past past (past perfect) tense is used to show that something happened in the past but before other events in the past. *Had* helps form the past past tense.

> After Johnson *had completed* her assignment, she relaxed at a party.

The shifting of tenses is frequently necessary, as is shown in this example:

> After Alexander the Great *had subdued* (past past) Thebes, he *conquered* (past) Persia. He then *went* (past) to Egypt, where he *founded* (past) the city of Alexandria. Alexandria *has been* (connecting) a major port since ancient times. Commerce *thrives* (present) there today.

## 3.8. Word Choice

The English language consists of more than 500,000 words, so you have many words to choose from. You should be choosing words that are short and specific. You should be avoiding long words, vague or abstract words, and clichés.

**3.8.1. Prefer short words to long ones.** Readers will understand you best if you use short words instead of long ones. The short list that follows gives samples of frequently used long words and their preferred shorter substitutes:

| INSTEAD OF WRITING | USE |
| --- | --- |
| assist | help, aid |
| communicate | write, tell, speak to |
| demonstrate | show |
| difficult | hard |
| discontinue | stop |
| disembark | get off |
| initiate | begin, start |
| modify, modification | change |
| prior to | before |
| subsequent to | after |
| terminate, termination | end |
| utilize | use |

**3.8.2. Prefer specific words to abstract ones.** Specific words name things individually, one at a time. Examples of specific words are *half-ton truck, Mount Everest,* and *radial arm saw.* Abstract words name qualities or ideas such as *beauty, culture, efficiency, loyalty,* and *wealth.*

Specific words are easy for the reader's mind to work with, because the concepts are simple and narrowly defined. Abstract words are harder for the reader to understand, because the things that abstract words stand for have no existence outside whatever existence the reader gives them.

The relationship between specific and abstract words can be further understood by comparing these sets:

Abstract: democracy
Specific:  Congress          voting booth

Abstract: old person
Specific:  wrinkled skin     thin and graying

Abstract: injury
Specific:  broken arm        dislocated shoulder

Abstract: color
Specific:  red               brown

**3.8.3. Avoid *al* and *ly* forms.** Stay away from words that end in *al* or *ly*. They are unclear and often unnecessary.

The word *exceptional* can mean that someone or something is exceptionally good or exceptionally bad. *Actual* can be scratched from your vocabulary with no noticeable loss. There's no point in writing, "The actual research took place last week." Research is research. When you insert the word *actual,* you allow readers to infer that there is fictitious, pretended, or simulated research.

Then there's the *ly* ending. Think about this sentence: "Relatively low doses are typically encountered at the ambient level." How relative? How typical?

And this one: "Protestantism effectively brought about a renewal of spiritual values." If something is brought about, the bringing about is effective. Ineffective changes are not brought about. They just don't happen.

Similarly, the word *really* serves little worthwhile purpose in written matter. People frequently use *really* when talking, in expressions such as "I really don't know" or "Really, now." Yet the word *really* isn't necessary in a sentence like this: "Accusations really flew thick and fast at the start of the trial." Reality is present; the word *really* doesn't make reality any more real. Worse, *really* carries with it the sound of childish exaggeration.

**3.8.4. Don't use clichés.** A cliché is usually criticized because it is a stale, overworked expression. The most important criticism is this: The meaning of a cliché is unclear.

What does it mean to say or write, "The tip of the iceberg" or "The bottom line"? If you say, "I feel comfortable with this assignment," do you mean that you like it or are just lukewarm about it? If you have a "meaningful relationship" with someone, are you talking about love, friendship, or just being neighborly?

We see and hear such statements so often that we become bored by them. Moreover, readers need something specific to relate to. Readers deserve to know the meaning of what you write.

## 3.9. Word Order

The most inflexible principle of English usage is this: The arrangement of words in a sentence determines the meaning of that sentence. The arrangement is known as *syntax,* which means word order.

How important is word order? Take a look at these two groups of words:

- interest earned on investments of $17,000
- interest of $17,000 earned on investments

Both contain the same words, but the word order is different—and so is the meaning.

Word order is serious business. As an example, watch what happens when the word *only* is moved around as is done here:

- *Only* my car ran out of gas yesterday. (No other car in the world did.)
- My *only* car ran out of gas yesterday. (I have but one car.)
- My car ran out of gas *only* yesterday. (Here two meanings are possible: "My car ran out of gas just yesterday" or "Yesterday was the one day my car ran out of gas," an idea that is made clearer in the next example.)
- My can ran out of gas yesterday *only*. (It happened but once.)

If word order is serious business, then it should have its funny side. It does, and the funny side is found when words get out of order. The technical term is *misplaced modifiers* and some examples are:

She had a cyst on the back of her neck that had to be surgically removed. (The cyst had to be removed, not her neck.)

They watched for thirty minutes at their leisure while the soldiers cavorted among the daisies that grew along the fence in perfect ignorance. (The soldiers cavorted in perfect ignorance, regardless of how the daisies grew.)

# CHAPTER 4

# THE SPECIAL TREATMENT OF WORDS AND NUMBERS

This chapter covers these subjects: how to use abbreviations, what to capitalize, how to show titles of works, how to assign special treatment to words and terms, and how to use numbers in your writing.

## 4.1. Abbreviations

If you must use an abbreviation, explain it to your reader. Write the term out in full on first use and show the abbreviation in parentheses: "Did you know that more than a dozen organizations use the same abbreviation as the American Medical Association (AMA)?" From then on you may use the abbreviation in its shortened form.

Other principles governing the use of abbreviations are these:

- Write them as you would say them. "A registered nurse" becomes "*an* RN," not "a RN." The pronunciation is "an are-en."

- Don't drop articles (*a, an, the*). If you would spell out "The United States Department of Agriculture," then the abbreviation is written as "the USDA."
- Don't begin a sentence with an abbreviation. Spell it out if it leads off the sentence or recast the sentence so that the abbreviation is inside the sentence.

## 4.2. Capitalization

**4.2.1. Capitalization—general.** *To capitalize* means to capitalize the first letter of a word.

CROSS-REFERENCES: For the capitalization of titles of works, see section 4.5.2. For the treatment of personal names, see section 4.3.1.

**4.2.2. Buildings and rooms.** Capitalize names of buildings and rooms:

```
The president's wife spoke to him in the Oval
Office of the White House.
```

```
A sinister connotation was attached to Room 101.
```

**4.2.3. The Deity.** All references to the Deity are capitalized:

```
God is the One who sustains us.
```

Expressions such as these are also capitalized: *Allah, Holy Ghost, Jehovah, Son of God.*

**4.2.4. First words.** Capitalize the first word of a complete sentence in these uses: when the sentence appears by itself, appears after a colon, is a quotation, or is in parentheses by itself. Do not capitalize the first word of a complete sentence that appears in parentheses or dashes inside another sentence.

```
The general decided upon one plan.


The general pondered this question:  Should we

attack at dawn?


To the general's command, "We'll attack at dawn,"

they all said, "Nuts."


Collisions between the classes of the old society

furthered the development of the proletariat.

(There were many such collisions.)


Collisions between the classes of the old society

(there were many such collisions) furthered the

development of the proletariat.


Collisions between the classes of the old society

--there were many such collisions--furthered the

development of the proletariat.
```

**4.2.5. Geographical areas and directions.** Nouns that name geographical areas are usually capitalized. Adjectives and descriptive terms that refer to those areas are usually not capitalized.

```
the Arctic; arctic climate

North Atlantic; northern Atlantic

Baja California

southern California

Middle West; Midwest; a midwesterner

Tennessee-Tombigbee Waterway; the waterway
```

Directions, such as *south*, are not capitalized, but the word *South* is capitalized when referring to an area of the country.

```
They lived in the South until drought struck;

then they pulled up stakes and traveled west.
```

**4.2.6. Groups of people.** Capitalize the names of specific national, racial, or similar groups. Examples are *Cheyenne Indians, Jew, Mormon, Hispanic, Negro, Italian,* and *Asian.*

Do not capitalize names based only on color, size, or local usage. Examples are *black, highlander, redneck,* and *white.*

In a class by itself is *native American,* not *Native* (capitalized), for American Indian.

**4.2.7. Organizations and events.** The full name of an organization or event is capitalized. Adjectives, short forms, and descriptive terms are not.

```
American Historical Association; the association

Hudson's Bay Company; the company

Battle of the Little Bighorn; the battle

United States Congress; the Ninety-ninth Congress;

     Congress; congressional

World Wildlife Fund; the fund

English 105.  Introduction to Beowulf; the course;

     the class

the Great Depression; the depression

the Ku Klux Klan; the Klan
```

**4.2.8. Periods of time.** Named periods are capitalized: *the Stone Age, the Christian Era, the Reformation, the Gilded Age.*

Numerically designated periods are not capitalized: *the nineteenth century, the sixties.*

A day (*Sunday*) is capitalized as is a month (*January*). A season (*spring*) is not capitalized.

CROSS-REFERENCES: For the writing of dates, see section 4.4.5. For the writing of years, see section 4.4.12.

**4.2.9. Political areas.** Words such as *city, county, state* are capitalized after a noun and not capitalized before it. As examples: *New York City,* but *the city of New York; Washington State,* but *the state of Washington.*

**4.2.10. Titles and offices of persons.** A title is capitalized when it immediately precedes a personal name: "In 1942, Major General Dwight Eisenhower headed the war plans division of the U.S. general staff."

A title need not be capitalized when it follows a personal name. Thus it is acceptable to write, "Franklin Delano Roosevelt, president of the United States." Neither would it be wrong to capitalize *president* in the example just given. Other examples are:

```
President Roosevelt; the president of the United
States; the president; presidential; the Roosevelt
administration


Prime Minister Margaret Thatcher; Prime Minister
Thatcher; Margaret Thatcher, prime minister of
Great Britain; the prime minister


General Ulysses S. Grant, commander in chief of
the Union army; General Grant; the commander in
chief; the general


Chairman of the Board Lee Iacocca; Lee Iacocca,
the chairman of the board; the chairman


Pope John Paul II; the pope
```

## 4.3. Names

CROSS-REFERENCE: This section deals with the names of people and vehicles. For the use of names of other entities, see section 4.2 on capitalization.

**4.3.1. Personal names.** Capitalize names and initials of persons:

```
Gloria Steinem          T. S. Eliot

JFK                     Jean-Paul Sartre

St. Thomas Aquinas      Mary of Burgundy
```

Some foreign names are capitalized differently than American names. Good guides to the correct spelling and capitalization of any name, American or foreign, are *Webster's New Biographical Dictionary*, *Who's Who*, and *Who's Who in America*.

A comma is not necessary between *Jr.* and the name it follows. Either of the following styles is acceptable.

```
Edward Martindale, Jr., took over the company
upon the death of his father.
```

```
Edward Martindale Jr. took over the company upon
the death of his father.
```

No comma is used between a name and its roman numeral:

```
Pope Clement VII refused to annul the marriage
between Henry VIII and Catherine of Aragon.
```

```
The letter was addressed to Henry W. Jaquith III.
```

A comma is used between a person's name and any degrees or affiliations:

```
As an attorney, the president could have signed
his name Abraham Lincoln, Esq.
```

Anthony Barbieri, LL.D., Ph.D., will give the
keynote speech.

A nickname or characterizing word or phrase used
in place of a person's name is capitalized. Quotation
marks or underlining are not used.

the Great Emancipator

the Swedish Nightingale

A nickname used with a person's name is placed in
quotation marks:

George Herman ("Babe") Ruth

Huey Long, "the Kingfish"

**4.3.2. Vehicles.** Underlining is used for the names
of ships, spacecraft, and human-made satellites. Underlining is not used with the names of cars and trains.
In addition, underlining is not used with abbreviations
such as *SS* or *HMS*, designations of class or make, and
names of space programs.

With the purchase of a Cadillac Seville, they
felt that they had really arrived.

The space shuttle <u>Challenger</u> carried with it the
<u>Westar 6</u> communications satellite.

Pentagon officials wanted to buy more C-5 Galaxy
jets.

The Burlington Zephyr was the world's first

```
mainline train powered by a diesel-electric
locomotive.
```

```
An aircraft carrier such as the USS John F.
Kennedy provides the main striking power of
the surface fleet.
```

## 4.4. Numbers

**4.4.1. Numbers—general.** In general, spell out numbers from one through ninety-nine. As examples, *man of fifty-two, seventy-sixth birthday, size ten dress, journey of seventeen miles,* but *100th birthday, 227 students.*

In addition, treat like subjects alike. That is, if you must use numerals for one of the references to a subject, then use numerals for all references to that subject.

```
A sample of 750 essays was selected from the top
quarter and the bottom half for each of nine
topics assigned; 683 essays were written on the
first four topics, but only 67 on the last five.
```

Also, do not use numerals at the start of a sentence. Either use numerals inside the sentence, or spell out the number at the start.

**4.4.2. Clarity and combinations of numbers.** When several numbers appear before a noun, confusing appearances can be avoided by using words for some and numerals for others.

```
The attack began when the two 3,000-man regiments
surged toward each other.
```

Sometimes the solution is to rewrite the sentence. Either of the following is acceptable, but the second version's consistent use of numerals makes it easier to grasp:

```
In the first group of twelve hundred, 300 were
questioned repeatedly.


In the first group, 300 of the 1,200
were questioned repeatedly.
```

In any event, quick comprehension is not gained by writing: "In the first group of 1,200, 300 were questioned repeatedly."

**4.4.3. Clock time.** Clock time is usually expressed as numerals, especially when the exact minute is important. A colon with no space on either side of it separates the hour from the minutes. The abbreviations *a.m.* and *p.m.* may be lowercased or capitalized and are punctuated with periods but no internal space:

```
Their flight departed at 3:19 p.m.


All participants completed testing in 2 hours and
27 minutes.
```

Words and not numerals are usually used for even, half, and quarter hours:

```
They ate dinner every night at seven.


The bridge is closed from midnight until noon.
```

**4.4.4. Compound numerical adjectives before a noun.**
When using a number to form an adjective before a noun, join the parts of the adjective with a hyphen:

```
Employees liked the four-day work week.


Congress approved a five-cent-per-bottle tax.
```

**4.4.5. Dates.** All of the following are correct forms for writing dates.

```
Someone will be appointed to arrange the May 1987

convention.


The society's next convention will convene on

May 21, 1987.


The May 21, 1987, convention has been

rescheduled.


The May 21, 1987 convention has been rescheduled.
```

**4.4.6. Inclusive numbers.** An inclusive number is written with a hyphen:

```
The Russo-Finnish War was fought during the winter

of 1939-1940.
```

**4.4.7. Indefinite, large, and round numbers.** Indefinite, large, and round numbers are usually spelled out:

```
Because he was a pessimist who considered himself

unlucky, he expected thirteen million things to go

wrong.
```

```
In a good year he sold five hundred head of
cattle.
```

Some numbers are better seen if numerals are used along with the words *million* or *billion*.

```
The population of the United States is 230
million.
```

```
Our planet earth is at least 4.5 billion years
old.
```

When there is a need to be specific, use numerals, and use a comma between thousands. As examples: *16,475; 1,212; 2,065,543.*

**4.4.8. Money.** When writing about money, cents are carried to two decimal places when there is a need to be specific. In addition, when you spell out the number, also spell out the unit of currency.

```
$3.25                    $4.00 worth of candy
$0.87 or 87 cents        $410 net loss
five dollars             $300,000
```

Amounts of money of a million dollars or more are partly spelled out. The reason is to avoid excessive strings of zeros. Note that the dollar sign comes before the numeral and not where the word *dollars* would fall:

```
Investments totaled $11 million for the year, and
sales amounted to $6 million.
```

```
The company's net worth is $1.25 billion.
```

**4.4.9. Percentages.** The word *percent* is used in text. The percent symbol (%) is used in tables.

**4.4.10. Spelled-out numbers: how to write.** When writing whole numbers, use a hyphen to connect a word ending in *y* to another word. As examples: *twenty-first, twenty-one.*

When writing fractions, use a hyphen unless *a* or *an* takes the place of the number *one.* As examples: *one and one-half years old; year and a half old.*

Plurals of numbers are written the same as plurals of other nouns.

```
They came in twos and threes.

He is a man in his forties.
```

**4.4.11. Time span and the apostrophe.** The apostrophe is used with time span in constructions like these:

```
Some people expect two weeks' pay for one day's

work.
```

**4.4.12. Years.** Years are best expressed as numerals. When the abbreviations *B.C.* or *A.D.* are used, they are capitalized. A space is placed between the year and the abbreviation. Note that *B.C.* follows the year; *A.D.* comes before:

```
Our best year was 1976.
```

```
Gaius Caesar, a grandson of Augustus, was born in

20 B.C. and died in A.D. 4.
```

However, *A.D.* may appear after the time period in this type of construction:

```
Disease struck the village in the second

century A.D.
```

When adding a prefix to a year, do so with a hyphen.

```
Her novel was definitely a pre-1950 epic.
```

## 4.5. Titles of Works

**4.5.1. Titles of works—general.** The word *works* refers to printed matter and works in the visual and performing arts. Underlining or quotation marks are used with these titles. For titles of printed matter that are on microfilm or microfiche, treat those titles as if they were on printed matter.

**4.5.2. Capitalization of titles of works.** The capitalization of titles of works is not consistent throughout the many publications printed in this country. Nevertheless, capitalization in your writing should be consistent, that is, the same throughout. Therefore, all titles of works that you write about should be capitalized according to this principle:

Capitalize the first and last word of a title and all other words except articles (*a, an, the*); prepositions (words such as *to, in, with, through*); and conjunctions (words such as *for, and, but*). Capitalize any word that begins the subtitle, even if the word is an article, preposition, or conjunction.

**4.5.3. Books, magazines, and newspapers.** Underlining is used for titles of complete documents such as books, booklets, brochures, bulletins, magazines, manuals, newsletters, newspapers, pamphlets, and scholarly journals.

```
Finely crafted prose can be found in the book

The Lives of a Cell:  Notes of a Biology Watcher.


Protection as the ideal solution is emphasized in

the report Oil Spill Response Planning for the

Greater San Francisco Bay Area.


Newsweek regularly carries a special section

aimed at college students.
```

EXCEPTIONS: Underlining is not used to label *diaries*, *personal journals*, *letters*, or *memos*. These expressions are simply lowercased.

CROSS-REFERENCE: The Bible and its books are treated according to the instructions in section 4.5.12.

**4.5.4. Articles, essays, parts of a book, short stories, speeches, and unpublished works.** Quotation marks are placed around titles of works in these categories: articles, essays, chapters or appendixes in a book, lectures, speeches, papers read at a meeting, and unpublished works such as theses and dissertations.

```
Yukio Mishima's story "Three Million Yen" has a

high shock value.
```

```
One of the most frequently anthologized essays is
George Orwell's "Shooting an Elephant."


The chapter "Geology and Ourselves" begins on
page 4.


Please refer to appendix A, "Questionnaire
Summaries."


Dr. Bryan gave the conference's keynote address,
"Subliminal Communication Techniques."


For the most complete treatment of the subject,
see John Thompson's thesis, "The Settlement
Geography of the Sacramento-San Joaquin Delta,
California."
```

EXCEPTIONS: Quotation marks are not used with words such as *chapter, table of contents, preface,* or *bibliography.* It is only necessary to write, "In chapter 4, Harbrace began a lengthy explanation of . . ."

**4.5.5. Acts, treaties, and laws.** Formal titles of acts, treaties, and laws are capitalized, not underlined, and not placed in quotation marks. Incomplete titles may be lowercased. As examples: *Twenty-first Amendment,* but *the amendment; Monroe Doctrine,* but *the doctrine; Second Five-Year Plan,* but *the plan.*

When referring to the Constitution of the United States, the short form *Constitution* is capitalized.

**4.5.6. Legal cases.** The complete title—plaintiff, *v.* (versus), and defendant—of a legal case is underlined. Also underlined are shortened references to the same case.

```
This decision was rendered in Pells v. Brown.


The appellate court again referred to the Pells

case.


On appeal, Pells was cited frequently.
```

If you have to cite many legal documents, see the Harvard Law Review Association's *A Uniform System of Citation.*

**4.5.7. Musical works and poetry.** Quotation marks are used with titles of short poems and short musical works.

```
The requirement is to memorize Frost's poem

"Stopping by Woods on a Snowy Evening."


Portions of the song "Ach du lieber Augustin"

can be heard in a suite by the composer John

Alden Carpenter.
```

Underlining is used with the titles of long musical works and long poems. A long musical work is a work such as an opera, oratorio, symphony, or concerto. A long poem is one that could be published as a book by itself.

```
Interest in Chaucer's Canterbury Tales remains

high today.



Handel died shortly after conducting a charity

concert of the Messiah.
```

In a paper in which long and short works are mentioned, underlining may be used for the titles of both.

Many musical works do not have descriptive titles. Instead, these works are identified by the name of their form plus a number or key signature. These titles are not placed in quotation marks and are not underlined.

```
C-sharp Minor Quartet

Concerto No. 3

Piano Quartet, op. 25
```

### 4.5.8. Movies and plays. Underlining is used for the titles of movies and plays.

```
Neil Simon's California Suite is a group of

one-act plays.



The movie The Name of the Rose is based on the

book of the same name.
```

The names of internal parts are not underlined, not placed in quotation marks, and not capitalized. The number of the internal part is written as a roman or arabic numeral; more formal styles use roman numerals. An alternative is to spell out the number.

```
The climax occurred in act 2, scene 4.


The climax occurred in act II, scene IV.


The climax occurred in the fourth scene of the

second act.
```

**4.5.9. Radio and television programs.** When referring to radio and television programs, series' titles are underlined, and the titles of individual episodes are placed in quotation marks.

```
"On with the Dance" was a favorite episode in

Upstairs, Downstairs.
```

**4.5.10. Paintings and sculptures.** Underlining is used for the titles of paintings, sculptures, drawings, and similar works of art.

```
Leonardo Da Vinci's Mona Lisa is probably the

most famous portrait ever painted.


Red Petals is a mobile by Alexander Calder.
```

**4.5.11. Figures and tables.** When referring to figures and tables in text, do not use underlining or quotation marks, and there is no need to capitalize the words *figure* and *table*.

```
These data are displayed in table 8.


Please consult figure 2 for an overview of this

trend.
```

**4.5.12. Sacred works.** The titles of sacred works and their parts are capitalized. Neither underlining nor quotation marks are used.

```
The Bible, the Koran, and the Talmud are the
world's most revered books.
```

```
The editors were able to reduce the length of
Genesis by cutting out a lot of repetition.
```

## 4.6. Words and Terms

**4.6.1. To add emphasis or irony.** Underlining is sometimes used to add emphasis:

```
Brandon demanded to know exactly what Bragg was
doing.
```

The use of underlining to add emphasis should be limited to single words or short expressions. When complete sentences or whole passages are underlined, the technique is overworked and is no longer effective.

Underlining is not necessary when the emphasis is added structurally, that is, by writing the passage to achieve emphasis:

```
Brandon commanded Bragg to report on his
activities.  Bragg's report was to contain exact
statements and omit vague or misleading remarks.
```

CROSS-REFERENCE: Use of the exclamation point to add emphasis is covered in section 5.3.4.

To add irony, use quotation marks:

Studs Terkel had to interview many veterans for his book on the "good" war.

They had to destroy the village in order to "save" it.

**4.6.2. To show rhyme schemes.** Underlining is used to show rhyme schemes; commas separate verses.

The English or Shakespearian sonnet rhymes abab, cdcd, efef, gg. The Spenserian variation is abab, bcbc, cdcd, ee.

**4.6.3. Use of *so-called*.** Quotation marks or underlining are not used when an expression is introduced with *so-called* or similar term.

He was the president's so-called fair-haired boy.

He insisted on naming his first son John.

Wyatt Earp is known as one of the participants in the gunfight at the OK Corral.

**4.6.4. Slang.** Slang is not part of the language of term papers unless you are writing *about* slang. If that is the case, then put quotation marks around the slang expression:

To a hobo, lice are "pants rabbits."

**4.6.5. Foreign words and phrases.** Do not use foreign words and phrases just to show off. If an unfamiliar foreign term is necessary, underline it:

```
To secure the best price for his efforts, he

turned his work over to a commissionnaire.
```

When quoting from a foreign language, copy all accents and other marks as they appear in the original: *abréger, soupçonner, detrás, riña, säuberlich*. If your typewriter does not have such marks, write them in by hand.

**4.6.6. Words as words; letters as letters.** When you write about a letter, word, or term, underline it:

```
The word oral should not be used to refer to

written language.
```

```
Rare is the word that begins with a q without a

u following.
```

The definition of an underlined word is placed in quotation marks:

```
Oral means "of the mouth."
```

A letter used as a shape is not underlined:

```
An A-frame cabin sat upon the hillside.
```

```
Lab specimens were flushed down a V-shaped trough.
```

To show the spelling of a word, place a hyphen between each letter:

```
In England, the spelling is with a u:

c-o-l-o-u-r.
```

**4.6.7. Plurals of underlined terms.** The plurals of underlined terms are treated according to these rules: (1) the singular form is underlined, and (2) the added *s* or *es* is not:

```
They bought ten Chronicles and Timeses.


Too many ands in writing sound odd.
```

An apostrophe helps prevent misreading of the plural form of letters treated as letters:

```
The computer printout was speckled with a's and

i's.
```

Omit the apostrophe if meaning is clear without it:

```
He lectured on the seven Ms of weight control--

METHOD, MEANING . . .


Campuses were scenes of unrest during the 1960s.
```

# CHAPTER 5

# PUNCTUATION

This chapter covers these uses of punctuation: punctuation that introduces, punctuation that separates, ending punctuation, punctuation that shows possession (use of the apostrophe), and punctuation that joins words (use of the hyphen).

To use the chapter, first decide what punctuation purpose you are trying to serve, what problem it is that you are trying to solve. As an example, if you have to punctuate a series of items such as *a*, *b*, and *c*, then look under the heading "To Separate Items in a Series." The information there will show you what punctuation mark to use.

In addition, these three terms and their definitions apply to instructions given in this chapter:

Clause.   A group of words containing a verb.
Phrase.   A group of words not containing a verb.
Sentence element.   A word, phrase, or clause.

## 5.1. Punctuation That Introduces

**5.1.1. Introductory punctuation—general.** Punctuation is used to separate an introductory sentence element from the main part of the sentence. The introductory element may be as short as a transitional word or phrase or as long as a complete clause.

Punctuation is also used to introduce a question, a statement, or a series. In addition, punctuation is used with introductory expressions such as *the following* and *that is*.

Regardless of where used, the purpose of introductory punctuation is to make the reader pause, to say to the reader, "Hey! Something's coming."

CROSS-REFERENCE: Introductory punctuation with quotations is covered in section 6.4.1.

**5.1.2. To mark off a transitional word or phrase.** A comma follows most transitional words or phrases. A comma is used whether the transition appears at the start of a sentence or after a semicolon:

```
Legally, neither party had the right to solicit
campaign funds.
```

```
On the other hand, the word become has a totally
different meaning.
```

```
Neither the city nor its residents are well
served by a governing process that leaves the
council in doubt about residents' views; of
course, the views of business and industry should
be heard too.
```

No comma is needed if you can read smoothly from the transition into the rest of the sentence:

```
At noon all activity stops except for a siesta.


During the past several years production levels

at the Fontana facilities have been hard hit by

increasing levels of foreign imports.
```

**5.1.3. To mark off an introductory clause.** A clause is a group of words that contains a verb.

Use a comma to separate an introductory clause from the main part of the sentence. In addition, use a comma with an introductory clause that follows a semicolon:

```
To obtain reliable information about enrollment

in colleges, a three-part survey was conducted.


Before launching into these matters, counselors

need to think about planning fieldwork on a

day-to-day basis.


For years he lived in New York; although he never

tired of the pace of the city, he longed for his

hometown of Springfield on many occasions.
```

An introductory clause in the second half of a compound sentence may be punctuated according to either style shown here. According to the first style, a comma appears before and after the introductory clause. In the second style, a comma appears after the clause:

```
Johnston's advance halted at the ridge, and, when
enemy fire had slackened, the assault gathered
new momentum.
```

```
Johnston's advance halted at the ridge, and when
enemy fire had slackened, the assault gathered
new momentum.
```

Two introductory clauses joined by *and* are punctuated in this manner:

```
Because they arrived late and because they had to
get up early the next morning, they did not
attend the evening seminar.
```

**5.1.4. To introduce a series.** A colon can be used to introduce a series:

```
The document covered issues in four areas:
safety, energy, capital formation, and
international trade.
```

A colon is not necessary when the series is worked into the sentence in this manner:

```
The document covered issues in the four areas of
safety, energy, capital formation, and
international trade.
```

**5.1.5. To introduce a statement.** Use a colon to end one sentence while introducing a statement or series of statements.

```
League officials enforced this rule:  Anyone
caught using drugs would be immediately suspended.


League officials enforced these rules:  Anyone
caught using drugs would be immediately suspended;
suspension is for life; and the suspended player
may appeal after a two-year waiting period.
```

**5.1.6. To introduce a question.** Use a colon when a complete sentence leads up to a question. Otherwise, use a comma:

```
Committee members asked this question:  When
would covert operations end?


Committee members wondered, When would covert
operations end?


The date was given as May 17, 1563, but by what
calendar?
```

**5.1.7. Punctuation with *as follows* or *the following*.** A colon is used after *as follows* or *the following*:

```
Attributes of science include the following:  a
structured discipline or body of knowledge; a way
of acquiring new knowledge; an interesting avenue
of personal fulfillment; and a social, economic,
and cultural influence.
```

**5.1.8. Punctuation with expressions such as *for example, namely, such as,* and *that is*.** Intoductory expres-

sions such as *for example, namely, such as,* and *that is*
are punctuated according to these guidelines: (1) The
expression is *preceded* by a comma or no punctuation
if the break in continuity is a minor one but by a
semicolon or a dash if the break is major; (2) the
expression is *followed* by a comma or no punctuation:

```
An introductory expression such as for example is
punctuated according to the guidelines given here.
```

```
Planners should consider any of the various
sources of curriculum design, for example, the
state framework.
```

```
Planners should consider the various sources of
curriculum design; for example, the state
framework is very helpful.
```

```
Research was performed for each basic industry,
namely, agriculture, manufacturing, mining, and
transportation.
```

```
Philosophers agree about the success of her major
achievement--that is, her ability to explain Greek
thought in simple terms.
```

The expression and the element it introduces may
be enclosed in dashes or parentheses:

```
The Sundesert Plant--that is, Project 4198--is
planned for Riverside County.
```

```
Other modes of organization (namely, attitude,

conceptual scheme, process, and skill or delivery

system) are commonly advocated.
```

**5.1.9. Capitalization after introductory punctuation.**
Capitalize a complete sentence that follows introductory punctuation. For examples, see section 4.2.4. for the capitalization of first words.

Do not capitalize the first letter of a list of items that does not make up a complete sentence:

```
The report focused on five main areas:  (1) data

relevant to market factors; (2) socioeconomic

data; (3) cost factors; (4) institutional

constraints; and (5) a statistical review.
```

## 5.2. Punctuation That Separates

**5.2.1. Punctuation that separates—general.** This section deals with punctuation to separate items within a sentence. The marks used are the comma, the dash, the parentheses, and the semicolon.

CROSS-REFERENCE: At the end of a sentence the marks of separation are the period, the question mark, and the exclamation mark. These are dealt with in section 5.3.

**5.2.2. To punctuate an interjection.** An interjection is a word or phrase inserted into a sentence for emphasis. Commas are frequently used with interjections:

```
Perhaps, however, the greatest attraction is the

friendliness and hospitality that exemplify

Texans everywhere.
```

At the level of etiquette, then, rules provide reasons for doing one thing rather than another.

The president's credibility, consequently, was seriously damaged.

When there is no break in continuity and no reason to pause while reading, commas may be omitted from around the interjection. In the following sentence, commas are not needed around *therefore*:

He therefore decided to seize Polish and Swedish possessions on the Baltic coast.

**5.2.3. To separate for clarity or ease of reading.** A comma should be used for the sake of clarity in constructions like these:

To Mary, Jones was a hard person to understand.

The morning after, the drunk went away forever.

She recognized the man who entered the room, and gasped.

A comma should be used to make the reader's task easier in sentences like these:

The squad marched in, in single file.

Whatever is, is good.

A comma is not needed in this type of sentence:

They recognized that that solution was the wrong one.

**5.2.4. To separate adjectives before a noun.** A comma is used between coordinate adjectives, that is, adjectives of equal rank before a noun.

```
Four of them spent the night in a large, cold
house.
```

```
His remarks carried all the sincerity of a shrewd,
scheming politician.
```

A comma is not used when the adjectives are not coordinate:

```
The attacker used a heavy steel pipe.
```

```
She took her bath in an old porcelain tub.
```

Noncoordinate adjectives—the instances in which you do not use a comma—can be spotted in two ways. First, if you insert *and* the result sounds awkward: "a heavy and steel pipe." Second, if you reverse the adjectives, the result again sounds awkward: "a steel heavy pipe."

No comma is used between the final adjective and the noun. As an example, the punctuation of this sentence is wrong: "Four of them spent the night in a large, cold, house." No comma is needed between *cold* and *house*.

CROSS-REFERENCE: To join adjectives before a noun, see sections 5.5.2, 5.5.3, 5.5.5, and 5.5.6.

**5.2.5. To separate items in a series.** In a series of three or more elements, the elements are separated by commas:

The method was accurate, simple, and inexpensive.

Educated, devout, and full of acrimony, he dipped his pen in vinegar and wrote a letter of hate.

Commas are not used when the elements are joined by conjunctions:

The survey reported on the three basic industries of agriculture and mining and manufacturing.

Semicolons are often desirable to separate long series of elements, and semicolons are usually necessary to separate elements that contain commas or other internal punctuation. In the first example below, the semicolons could be replaced with commas. In the second example, the semicolons are necessary.

These philosophies include an underlying knowledge of learning theories; a view of the society and how learners are served with an assessment of needs; and overall goals and objectives that are consistent with the requirements of education.

Persons consulted were Wilbur R. Moore, Chairman, Riverside Elementary School Curriculum Committee; Mary Johannes, Carbon County Unified School District; and Dorothy Chang, Office of the University Trustees, Springfield.

## 5.2.6. To mark off complementary or contrasting elements. Commas are used to mark off complementary or contrasting elements:

Such a code of ethics should be a document,
written in plain language, that clearly and
precisely applies to real situations.

Many environmentalists were pleased, rather than
alarmed, at the long list of species on the
protected list.

That may explain, but it does not excuse, a
violation of the law.

The more they read the law, the more they became
confused.

## 5.2.7. To punctuate contrasting elements featuring *not*. Commas are used to mark off contrasting elements featuring *not*:

Energy concerns, not environmental issues, held
the spotlight.

Corporate policy must follow government policy,
not the other way around.

The sample size must be adjusted to survey
requirements, not only to provide an adequate
sample, but also to establish sampling error.

**5.2.8. To punctuate a compound sentence.** A compound sentence consists of two simple sentences joined by a conjunction. Typical conjunctions are *and, but, for, or, so,* or *yet.* A comma comes before the conjunction:

```
Hayes looked for an answer to the spoils system,

for an answer was necessary.


Serious cases called for alerts to be reported as

quickly as possible, and wardens were trained to

recognize these cases.
```

A comma is not needed in a short compound sentence where the elements are closely related:

```
They laughed and they cried.


Thomas ran and his wife walked to the bus stop.
```

For a more abrupt break than that provided by a comma, you may use a semicolon to separate the parts of a compound sentence. No conjunction is used:

```
California has several standards covering required

medical services; these standards mandate

different protective services for different types

and sizes of businesses.
```

**5.2.9. To punctuate a sentence with a compound predicate.** Don't confuse a compound sentence with a compound predicate in a simple sentence. A compound sentence contains two or more subjects and predicates. A simple sentence with a compound predicate contains one subject with two things being said about it, that is, two predicates.

When the parts of a compound predicate are long, a comma helps separate them.

```
McQueen began by denouncing Spake's ungenerosity
and unfairness toward Robison, and then proceeded
to tear into and demolish Spake's overall
character.
```

```
The Khedive Ismail of Egypt had arrived at the
crest of his highly prosperous career by the end
of the 1860s, and had borrowed and spent his
nation into bankruptcy and financial ruin.
```

When the parts of a compound predicate are short, a comma may be used but is not necessary. In this next example, no comma is needed before *and*:

```
He acted in a large number of movies and wrote
several prize-winning plays.
```

**5.2.10. To mark off an essential element.** An essential element is one that cannot be removed from a sentence without changing the basic meaning of the sentence. An essential element is also called a *restrictive* element because it restricts, limits, defines, or identifies the word or sentence element it refers to. In other

words, a restrictive element is essential to the meaning
of the sentence. Therefore, the term *essential* is used
here.

In the following example, note these words: "that
flow out of the Wasatch Mountains."

> Rivers that flow out of the Wastach Mountains are
> flooding the Great Salt Lake.

If "that flow out of the Wasatch Mountains" is
removed, the sentence reads: "Rivers are flooding the
Great Salt Lake." Now we don't know which rivers
are meant. So that the reader can understand what's
being talked about, the element "that flow out of the
Wasatch Mountains" is provided, and it is essential to
the meaning of the sentence.

An essential element that appears as an introductory clause is set off from the rest of the sentence with
a comma. In this first example, the essential element is
"If we participate constructively in the policy-making
process." That essential element appears as an introductory clause, the mark of a clause being a group of
words that contains a verb; in this case the verb is
"participate." Accordingly, a comma follows the
element:

```
If we participate constructively in the

policy-making process, we can help obtain

responsible legislation.
```

Otherwise, no comma is necessary if the introductory essential element does not contain a verb. However, a comma may be used after any introductory

essential element for ease of reading. Either style of punctuation is appropriate in this next pair of examples. In them the essential element is "In our personal conduct"; without it, the sentence would be vague.

```
In our personal conduct we must set rigorous
standards.


In our personal conduct, we must set rigorous
standards.
```

CROSS-REFERENCE: For more help with punctuating introductory sentence elements, see sections 5.1.2. and 5.1.3.

Anywhere else in the sentence, in the middle or at the end, commas are not used with essential elements, whether or not the elements contain verbs.

For instance, the essential element in this next example is "that were at first rejected." Without it, the meaning of the sentence is too broad. Commas are not used.

```
All of Merton's ideas that were at first rejected
are now widely accepted.
```

Concerning this next example, if you removed the underlined title of the play, no one would know which play the sentence is referring to. Consequently, the title is essential, and commas are not used.

```
Shakespeare's play Romeo and Juliet is a tragedy.
```

This next example shows an essential element at the end of a sentence. The element is "in our personal conduct." Remove it, and the sentence could refer to anything. A comma is not used before "in."

```
We must set rigorous standards in our personal

conduct.
```

**5.2.11. To mark off a nonessential element.** A writer sometimes puts into a sentence an element—a word, phrase, or clause—that adds to the basic meaning of the sentence. This type of element provides descriptive detail useful to the reader. If this element is taken out of the sentence, the basic meaning remains unchanged. A word, phrase, or clause used in this manner is *nonessential*; that is, it is not essential to the basic meaning of the sentence. A nonessential element is also known as a *nonrestrictive* element.

An example of a nonessential element is the clause "which flows out of the Wasatch Mountains" in the following sentence:

Lost Creek, which flows out of the Wasatch Mountains, is a source of pleasure for anglers.

We know what creek the writer is talking about because it is named—Lost Creek. Therefore, the basic meaning of the sentence is this: "Lost Creek is a source of pleasure for anglers." The clause "which flows out of the Wasatch Mountains" is not essential to the basic meaning of the sentence.

Commas are used to set off nonessential elements whether the elements appear at the beginning of a sentence, in its middle, or at its end. In each of the examples that follow, if you removed the elements marked off by commas, the basic meaning of the sentence would remain unchanged.

```
Azevedo's Department Store, which opened only last
month, is doing a brisk business.
```

```
The regimental commander, Lieutenant Colonel
Roosevelt, ordered the charge.
```

```
The charge was ordered by Lieutenant Colonel
Roosevelt, the regimental commander.
```

```
We must serve to right racial wrongs, if we can
serve at all.
```

```
If we can serve at all, we must serve to right
racial wrongs.
```

**5.2.12. To mark off an explanatory element.** Explanatory elements may be marked off with any of the punctuation marks shown in the following examples. A comma provides the least degree of interruption.

```
It was claimed that the textbook, in its
discussion of the theory of evolution, violated
the plaintiff's right to free exercise of his
religion.
```

The student's attitude, generally speaking, determines what he or she will do autonomously.

Keetah had an important decision to make, whether to go outside or stay in the village of her ancestors.

Keetah had an important decision to make: whether to go outside or stay in the village of her ancestors.

They needed only one thing:  money.

He rebuked them for their spirit of revolt and even claimed--a new complaint this--that they had tried to murder him, his wife, and his eldest son.

Of the corporation's sales of $5.6 billion, about one third ($1.9 billion) came about because of international operations.

He was interested in concluding a durable peace that would help deliver to him the young lady of his wishes--beautiful and submissive.

Statistical data are presented later (see appendix A).

## 5.3. Ending Punctuation; Multiple Marks Together

**5.3.1. Ending punctuation and abbreviations.** A period is used after some abbreviations: *Dr., Mr., Mrs., Ms.*

Do not double the period when a sentence ends with an abbreviation:

```
He invaded Greece in 475 B.C.
```

**5.3.2. To end a statement.** A statement is neither exclamatory nor questioning. A statement ends with a period.

```
They settled in the Yolo farmlands and the Capay

hills.
```

```
The research needs to be analyzed.
```

**5.3.3. To end a question.** A direct question ends with a question mark:

```
They all wondered, How did this happen?
```

```
Could Moliere have phrased the passage more

cynically?
```

An indirect question ends with a period:

```
How this could happen was the question on
everyone's lips.
```

```
The real question is whether Moliere could have
phrased the passage more cynically.
```

**5.3.4. To end an exclamation.** An exclamation, out-cry, or emphatic comment ends with an exclamation mark. This mark should seldom, if ever, be used, especially in term papers.

```
He shouted, "Help!"
```

```
When they begged for mercy, he beat them harder
and showed no mercy!
```

**5.3.5. Ending punctuation not used.** Don't use a period at the end of a sentence within a sentence:

```
Her statement, "I was late because of a flat
tire," was not believed.
```

```
The sarcasm in his voice (you could hardly fail
to notice it) did not set well with the crowd.
```

```
The sarcasm in his voice--you could hardly fail
to notice it--did not set well with the crowd.
```

EXCEPTION: When an interior sentence calls for an exclamation mark or a question mark, these should be retained:

```
She cried--had she been crying all night?--and

the nurse went to her side.
```

**5.3.6. Multiple punctuation marks together.** When two different marks of punctuation could occur at the same location in a sentence, the stronger mark is used:

> Who shouted, "Run up the flag!" (No question mark at the end.)
>
> "Run up the flag!" was the shout. (No comma after "flag!")

The consecutive use of the same mark usually does not pose problems. For instance, commas to separate items in a series are standard, as in 1, 2, 3, and 4. However, the use of parentheses inside parentheses looks strange, and writers should work to avoid such combinations. And to prevent confusion, you should not use more than two dashes in a sentence.

The rules for punctuation with parentheses are these:

1. (When a complete sentence is enclosed in parentheses, place ending punctuation inside the parentheses, like this.)
2. When only part of a sentence is enclosed in parentheses (like this), place ending punctuation outside the parentheses (like this).

Some examples are:

```
The prisoner died.  (He had refused to eat.)


The prisoner died (the one who refused to eat).
```

Convert European date forms (28 Aug. 1983) to
conventional (Aug. 28, 1983).


Can anyone forget--or forgive--<u>Zardoz</u> (1974)?

**If required by sentence structure, other punctuation may follow a closing parenthesis:**

The rich Ukraine, including Kiev (the Orthodox
mother of all Russian cities), was ceded to
little Poland.


The rich Ukraine--including Kiev (the Orthodox
mother of all Russian cities)--was ceded to
little Poland.


Congressional investigators became concerned
about lost copies of the report (original and
final versions):  All of the copies had
mysteriously vanished during the night.


They used the European date form (28 Aug. 1983);
it should be converted to conventional (Aug. 28,
1983).

**Where an expression is underlined, the punctuation that immediately follows is treated similarly:**


Why were they talking about the <u>cosmos?</u>

## 5.4. Possession (Use of the Apostrophe)

**5.4.1. Possession—general.** You show possession in most instances by adding an apostrophe to a noun or by adding an apostrophe and an *s*. Often the choice is determined not by some rigid grammatical rule but by whether a word sounds right with one, two, or even three *s*'s tacked onto the end of it.

You can also show possession by using a personal pronoun such as *his* or *ours*.

**5.4.2. Singular noun not ending in *s*.** A singular noun not ending in *s* is made into a possessive by adding an apostrophe and an *s*: *man's, woman's, lion's den*.

**5.4.3. Singular noun ending in *s*.** A singular noun ending in *s* or with an *s* sound is made into a possessive by either (1) adding an apostrophe and an *s*, or (2) adding an apostrophe only. As examples: *proprietresses's jewels* or *proprietress' jewels; Berlioz's opera,* or *Berlioz' opera; Marx's theories,* or *Marx' theories; General Motors's profits, General Motors' profits.*

**5.4.4. Plural noun not ending in *s*.** Some plural nouns do not end in *s*. When forming the possessive of those nouns, add an apostrophe and an *s*: *men's, women's, children's, alumni's.*

**5.4.5. Plural noun ending in *s*.** Plural nouns ending in *s* need only the apostrophe to form the possessive: *states' rights, infants' lives, Joneses' life-style.*

**5.4.6. Noun ending in an *eez* sound.** To avoid awkward-sounding endings, an apostrophe without the *s* forms the possessive of a word ending with an *eez* sound: *Hercules' labors, Xerxes' troops, aborigines' traditions*.

**5.4.7. Compound nouns.** To form the possessive of a compound noun, add an apostrophe and an *s* to the element nearest the item possessed: *attorney general's opinion* (singular); *attorneys general's opinions* (plural); *brothers-in-law's tools* (plural).

**5.4.8. Alternative possession.** Alternative possession occurs when each noun individually possesses something. To show alternative possession, show possession on each noun: *Nixon's and Reagan's administrations; Gonzalez's and Koya's opinions*.

**5.4.9. Joint possession.** Joint possession occurs when the nouns together possess something. To construct a joint possession, show possession on the last noun: *soldiers and sailors' home; Green and Bronowski's theory*.

**5.4.10. Descriptive terms.** Apostrophes are not used with terms that are more descriptive than possessive: *citizens band radio; House of Representatives session*.

**5.4.11. Possessive pronouns.** An apostrophe is used when forming the possessive of pronouns such as these: *someone else's plans; anyone's guess; each other's notes; other's plans*.

An apostrophe is not used with *mine, our, ours,*

*your, yours, his, hers, its, their, theirs,* or *whose.* These terms show possession without the apostrophe.

In addition: Do not write *it's* ("it is") for the possessive *its.* Do not write *there* ("place") or *they're* ("they are") for the possessive *their.* Do not write *who's* ("who is") for the possessive *whose.* Do not write *you're* ("you are") for the possessive *your.*

## 5.5. Use of the Hyphen

**5.5.1. Hyphens—general.** Hyphens are used to join words, forming what are known as compound words. A dictionary is a good starting point for solving any problem with a compound word. A dictionary will often show if a word is hyphenated, written as a solid compound (such as *roughshod*), or formed as an open compound (such as *round lot*).

A dictionary is also helpful for questions concerning hyphens in the following forms: figures of speech (such as *stick-in-the-mud*); phrases adapted from a foreign language (such as *prima facie*); prefix combinations (involving, as examples, *all, anti, co, extra, intra, mis, multi, non, post, pre, pro, self, sub, super,* and *un*); more generally known scientific and technical terms; and so-called improvised compounds (such as *U-boat* and *H-bomb*).

**5.5.2. Hyphens for clarity.** Use hyphens to improve the clarity of your writing. Each of the following examples could be misread were it not for the hyphens in them.

```
They sailed on an American-flag ship.


Meals consisted of canned baby-food.


He bought a little-used car.
```

You may omit the hyphen when meaning is clear without it. In the following examples, no need exists to hyphenate "New Testament" and "Old Testament" (Ex. 1); "Lake Shore Drive" (Ex. 2); "child welfare" (Ex. 3); and "word processing" (Ex. 4).

```
1.  New Testament language is not as poetic as
    Old Testament language.
2.  The wealthy live in Lake Shore Drive mansions.
3.  County officials approved the child welfare
    plan.
4.  Bids were taken on a new word processing
    system.
```

You can avoid writing awkward or misleading prefixes by using hyphens. Ambiguity would exist without a hyphen in *un-ionized* (as compared to *unionized*) or *pre-position* (as compared to *preposition*). Similarly, hyphens are valuable in words such as *co-op* (as compared to *coop*), *re-sort* ("sort again" and not *resort*), and *re-treat* ("treat again" and not *retreat*).

In addition, doubled prefixes are easier to read if hyphens are used:

Let me re-redirect your attention to yesterday's testimony.

The sub-subcommittee began its work yesterday.

### 5.5.3. Hyphens with adjectives.
Use a hyphen between words that form an adjective immediately before a noun. Use no hyphen if the adjective appears elsewhere in the sentence. The pairs of examples shown here demonstrate the difference.

1.  Live Aid raised money for starving people in drought-stricken areas.
    Large parts of Africa are drought stricken.

2.  It is a large-scale project.
    The project is large scale.

3.  He despised get-it-done, make-it-happen thinking.
    He despised thinking that said get it done, make it happen.

4.  Testing was the subject of a U.S.-U.S.S.R. agreement.
    Testing was the subject of an agreement between the U.S. and the U.S.S.R.

The adjectives *long-lived* and *short-lived* are hyphenated wherever they appear:

```
It was a short-lived prophecy.

The prophecy was short-lived.
```

Hyphens are used with adjectives that begin with *best, better, ill, lesser, little,* or *well*:

```
She is a well-known performer.

They formulated an ill-advised policy.
```

*But* the hyphens are omitted when the adjective follows the noun:

```
She is very well known.

The policy is ill advised.
```

Adjectives that describe color are hyphenated:

```
The iron-gray ship slowly sailed into view.


To save money they settled for black-and-white

printing.
```

Compound adjectives—two or more words per adjective—are hyphenated as shown here:

```
The biggest establishment in town is the

Circus-owned 600-room Edgewater Hotel.


Water flowed today for the first time through the

Folsom Lake-East Side diversion project.


An old book dealt with the Herbert

Hoover-Department of Agriculture program.
```

CROSS-REFERENCE: For help with hyphenating numbers in adjectives, see section 4.4.4.

**5.5.4. Hyphens with nouns.** Hyphenated compound nouns, unlike adjectives before a noun, are hyphenated wherever they appear:

```
He is a manic-depressive.


He was diagnosed as being a manic-depressive

schizophrenic.


Dreyfuss served as a go-between.


Checkpoint Charlie was a go-between meeting

point.
```

**5.5.5. Hyphens not necessary.** Hyphens are not used with an *ly* ending:

```
It is a wholly owned subsidiary.


The signal came from a rapidly approaching ship.
```

In addition, you may omit hyphens from compounds inside quotation marks:

```
The city adopted a "prior use" ordinance years

ago.
```

**5.5.6. The suspensive hyphen.** When two or more words in a hyphenated compound have the same basic element and this element is mentioned in the last term only, a suspensive hyphen is used:

```
Old colleges are noted for their moss- and

ivy-covered walls.


Before opening an account, he checked the

long- and short-term interest rates.
```

**5.5.7. Hyphens with titles.** Use a hyphen with double- and triple-worded titles such as these:

```
He retired from his post as secretary-treasurer.


In an economy move, the organization created the

post of treasurer-manager.


She was promoted rapidly to the position of

editor-in-chief.
```

Titles with *vice* in them may be written without hyphens:

```
Vice President Andrew Johnson followed Lincoln.

The vice commander was promoted last week.
```

It is correct, however, to hyphenate *vice-presidency*.

A hyphen is used when *elect* or *designate* is suffixed to a title:

President-elect Wong called the meeting to order.

As ambassador-designate he was very careful with his remarks.

# CHAPTER 6

## QUOTATIONS

A quotation is a passage copied from the work of another writer. Quotations require the use of quotation marks (double or single), introductory punctuation (comma, colon, or none), ending punctuation (periods, question marks, or exclamation marks), and sometimes other marks such as ellipsis points, the dots that show omission.

Ways of using quotations are shown in this chapter.

### 6.1. Principles for Using Quotations

The nineteenth-century essayist Ralph Waldo Emerson spoke for many readers of any age when he wrote, "I hate quotations. Tell me what you know."[1]

To tell readers what you know, write your paper in your own words for the most part. When you use quotations, use few of them, and keep them short. Do not quote merely to fill up space or to show that you are well read: that fake use of quotations shows through quickly.

Writers of term papers generally find themselves in two situations where quotations are helpful, if not necessary. One situation concerns the writer of a paper that analyzes a literary work. That paper will have to contain occasional quotations selected for criticism and comment. The second situation involves the writer who wishes to clinch an argument by quoting an authority. In that case, the authority's words should be used to add to arguments already stated by the paper's author.

You might also want to use a quotation simply because you have come across a well-turned phrase that will add a little spice or humor to your paper. That use is permissible, too, provided you connect the quotation to your subject.

Anyway, for whatever reason you use quotations be certain that you always name your source to avoid plagiarism.

CROSS-REFERENCES: For methods of citing sources, see chapter 8. For plagiarism, see section 2.4.

## 6.2. Run-in or Indented?

**6.2.1. Run-in quotations—general.** One way to incorporate a quotation into text is to write it as part of the text itself. A quotation used in this manner is called a *run-in quotation*. Quotation marks are placed around a run-in quotation.

**6.2.2. Indented quotations—general.** A quotation may be treated separately from the text, as indented matter. A quotation displayed in this manner is called a *block-indented quotation* or a *block quotation*. Quotation marks are not placed around an indented quotation.

NOTE: Some handbooks call for the single-spacing of block-indented quotations. Those requirements should be limited to theses and dissertations, which are unique documents in many ways. Throughout the worlds of commercial and scholarly publishing, the standard requirement is to double-space all portions of the manuscript. In addition, double-spaced block-indented quotations make the typing and the spacing consistent throughout the term paper. Accordingly, this book recommends that block-indented quotations, as well as all other parts of the term paper, be double-spaced. To be safe, check with your instructor.

**6.2.3. Run-in prose quotations.** Short prose quotations, of less than approximately five typewritten lines, may be run into the text:

```
    As Rose says in his book on
computer-generated intelligence, "One of the
problems with this approach is that nobody really
knows very much about how the human mind works."2
Rose then goes on to describe the chemistry in
the brain that produces thinking.
```

**6.2.4. Block-indented prose quotations.** A block-indented prose quotation should be used in two instances: (1) when the number of typed lines is five or greater, and (2) when you are comparing quotations regardless of length. The following example shows the text that leads into a block-indented prose quotation:

The Epic of Gilgamesh, written about four thousand years ago, is a story of adventure, morality, and tragedy. The tale begins as the narrator introduces Gilgamesh:

I will proclaim to the world the deeds of Gilgamesh. This was the man to whom all things were known; this was the king who knew the countries of the world. He was wise, he saw mysteries and knew secret things, he brought us a tale of the days before the flood. He went on a long journey, was weary, worn-out with labour, returning he rested, he engraved on a stone the whole story.

When the gods created Gilgamesh they gave him a perfect body. Shamash the glorious sun endowed him with beauty, Adad the god of the storm endowed him with courage, the great gods made his beauty perfect, surpassing all others, terrifying like a great wild bull. Two thirds they made him god and one third man.[3]

To type a block-indented prose quotation, note these features of the preceding example: (1) Quadruple spacing is used above and below the quotation; (2) the quotation is indented five spaces from both left and right margins; (3) the quotation is typed double-spaced; (4) the first paragraph is not given additional indentation; and (5) subsequent paragraphs are indented an additional five spaces.

**6.2.5. Run-in poetry quotations.** A line or two of quoted poetry may be run into the text. When so done, the end of a line of poetry is marked by the slant bar (/), with one space on either side of the bar.

```
As Herrick wrote, "Gather ye Rose-buds while ye
may, / Old Time is still a flying."⁴
```

**6.2.6. Indented poetry quotations.** When more than two lines of poetry are quoted, the quotation is set off from the text. The portion quoted is centered on the page, with quadruple spacing above and below the quotation. Alignment of lines should represent the original as closely as possible.

```
             Thou sorrow, venom elf;
                Is this thy play,
          To spin a web out of thyself
                To catch a fly?
                  For why?⁵
```

If lines are too long to be centered on a page, as in Edgar Allan Poe's "The Raven," the quotation should

be indented from the left margin and the long lines
brought down and also indented:

```
Then, methought, the air grew denser, perfumed
       from an unseen censer
Swung by seraphim whose footfalls tinkled on
       the tufted floor.
"Wretch," I cried, "thy God hath lent thee--by
       these angels he hath sent thee."[6]
```

Indentation of quoted poetry should be uniform
throughout the paper. That is, if one quotation of
poetry is centered, then all should be centered. If one
quotation is too long to be centered and is therefore
indented from the left margin, then all quotations of
poetry should be indented the same amount.

Quotation marks are not used with block-indented
poetry unless the marks are part of the poem itself.
Quotation marks at the beginning of a line of poetry
are aligned with the first letter of the line above:

```
He holds him with his skinny hand,
"There was a ship," quoth he.
"Hold off! unhand me, grey-beard loon!"
Eftsoons his hand dropt he.[7]
```

## 6.3. Capitalization of Quotations

**6.3.1. Capitalization required.** Capitalize the first
letter of a complete quoted sentence, regardless of

length. See the samples in section 4.2.4, on the capitalization of first words.

**6.3.2. Capitalization not required.** A quoted sentence fragment worked into the text does not begin with a capital letter:

```
The chairwoman reported that "these safety

procedures worked" because of the skills and

dedication of employees.
```

**6.3.3. Changes to capitalization.** A lowercase letter in the original may be capitalized when quoted and when the structure of the text suggests the change. Note this sentence from Aldo Leopold's *A Sand County Almanac.*

> For us of the minority, the opportunity to see geese is more important than television, and the chance to find a pasque-flower is a right as inalienable as free speech.[8]

A major portion of that sentence can be quoted in this way, beginning with the second "the" in Leopold's version:

```
Aldo Leopold wrote, "The opportunity to see

geese is more important than television, and the

chance to find a pasque-flower is a right as

inalienable as free speech."
```

## 6.4. Punctuation of Quotations

**6.4.1. Introductory punctuation with quotations.** A comma is frequently used as the introductory mark with short quotations and following words such as *say, said, writes, wrote,* and *remarked*:

```
Ramirez wrote, "In this case, time is not of the
essence."
```

```
As Ramirez remarked, "In this case, time is not
of the essence."
```

An intervening statement after *said* or similar words does not do away with the need for the introductory comma:

```
Ramirez said more than once, "Time is not of the
essence."
```

A broken quotation takes commas in this manner:

```
"In this case," Ramirez said, "time is not of the
essence."
```

No comma is needed if the quotation is worked smoothly into the sentence:

```
The terse message was "Sighted sub, sank same."[9]
```

A colon may be used as the introductory mark with a quotation, regardless of length, made by a prominent person:

```
Gandhi said:   "Nonviolence is the first article
of my faith.   It is also the last article of my
creed."10
```

A colon is used to introduce an indented quotation:

```
In The Sea Around Us, Rachel Carson provides this
sensitive interpretation of her subject:
```

```
        The sea lies all about us.   The commerce
        of all lands must cross it.   The very
        winds that move over the lands have been
        cradled on its broad expanse and seek
        ever to return to it.   The continents
        themselves dissolve and pass to the sea,
        in grain after grain of eroded land.
        So the rains that rose from it return
        again in rivers.11
```

**6.4.2. Double marks or single?** Quoted words, phrases, or sentences run into text are enclosed in double quotation marks. Single quotation marks enclose quotations within run-in quotations; double marks are used for quotations within these; and so on:

```
"Fourteen days later," Harper wrote, "the regime
fell.  As he fled the capital, the emperor said,
'We will begin anew.  Mark my words.'"
```

Material set off from the text as an indented quotation is not enclosed in quotation marks. However, quoted matter within a block quotation is enclosed in quotation marks. To do so may require changing single marks to double or vice versa.

An example can be made of the following passage, which is from Margaret Craven's novel *I Heard the Owl Call My Name*. In the original, the bishop is speaking to a vicar, and the quotation marks are used thus:

> "It is an old village—nobody knows how old. According to the myth, after the great flood two brothers were the only human beings left alive in the world, and they heard a voice speak and it said, 'Come, Wolf, lend them your skin that they may go fleetly and find themselves a home.' And in the wolf's skin the brothers moved south until they came to a small and lovely valley on a river's edge."[12]

If you block indented that quotation, the opening double quote would drop off, and the interior single quote would be doubled. With an appropriate introductory statement, the passage would appear like this:

```
The young vicar remembered what his bishop had
told him of the village:
```

```
      It is an old village--nobody knows how
      old.  According to the myth, after the
```

great flood two brothers were the only
human beings left alive in the world,
and they heard a voice speak and it
said, "Come, Wolf, lend them your skin
that they may go fleetly and find
themselves a home." And in the wolf's
skin the brothers moved south until they
came to a small and lovely valley on a
river's edge.

### 6.4.3. Ending punctuation with quotations. Commas and periods are placed inside ending quotation marks:

See chapter 8, "The Wonderful Micromachines,"
which covers the subject thoroughly.

Everyone grows tired of a speaker who begins
every sentence with "You know."

He stood and said, "I will now recite Frost's
'Mending Wall.'"

Exclamation marks and question marks go inside
quotation marks if they are part of the original quotation. Otherwise, place them outside:

During Whitman's life, the poem that most
audiences wanted to hear him read was "O Captain!
My Captain!"

Many people are completely fed up with insincere
jerks who say, "Have a nice day"!

Tom asked, "Why will it take so long to debug the
machine?"

Why did Rawlings say, "It gives me a nauseous
feeling, because I'm not doing it"?

She stood, trembling before the class, and asked,
"May I be given another poem to recite other than
'Remembrance'?"

Colons, semicolons, and dashes are placed outside
of ending quotation marks:

The critic gave only one reason for liking Cyndi
Lauper's "Time after Time": It has a haunting
melody.

Poe's term for detective work was "ratiocination";
he used it often in referring to his stories.

CROSS-REFERENCE: More information on ending punctuation is provided in section 5.3.

**6.4.4. Quotation marks not used.** Quotation marks
are not used with indirect speech.

```
The consort said to his queen that their time was
running out.


Ivan told his chamberlains to stop asking why.


Every time the admiral was asked that question his
answer was no.


At this point we must pause and ask, What is the
fate of society?
```

**6.4.5. Showing corrections to quotations.** Sometimes it is necessary to show corrections of quotations. To do so, use square brackets, not parentheses:

```
"She'd never seen him [Wellington] until that
night."


"Despite the shelling, Bur[r]ington remained at
his post."
```

A misspelled word, a word wrongly used, or a grammatical error in the original may be shown by use of the word *sic* (meaning "so" or "thus"). No period comes after *sic*, because it is not an abbreviation. Brackets are placed around *sic*; the underlining of it is optional.

A typical use of *sic* is shown in this next example. There the word *authors* should be written without the apostrophe:

```
"Author's [sic] should get a little recognition

for their contributions."
```

**6.4.6. Adding emphasis to quotations.** If you wish to add emphasis to a word or words being quoted, underline them. The next step is to tell the reader that you did indeed add the emphasis. You can do this by one of two methods: (1) insert a comment in brackets directly after the underlined portion and inside quotation marks, or (2) insert a comment in parentheses directly after the quotation and outside the quotation marks:

```
"That mistrust is the most serious [underlining

added] obstacle in the way of reducing the

burdens caused by regulation."


"This spurred Spain to secure its old claim to

the empty land" (emphasis added).
```

If you wish to point out that the emphasis was in the original, you may use brackets or parentheses and expressions such as "emphasis in original." Better still, give the original author's name:

```
"Only seventeen of the giant condors are known to

be alive" (emphasis in original).


"Only seventeen [Ryan's emphasis] of the giant

condors are known to be alive."
```

# 6.5. Showing Omissions from Quotations

**6.5.1. Omissions and ellipsis points.** You may choose to omit part of a quotation. The omission is the *ellipsis*, and the ellipsis is replaced with *ellipsis points*. Ellipsis points are periods typed on the line.

**6.5.2. Ellipsis points to replace part of a sentence.** Three ellipsis points are used to replace part of a sentence. A space is placed before the first point, between each point, and after the third point. Adjacent punctuation need not be retained unless necessary to the meaning of the original. In the following sentence, reprinted here in its entirety, note the words "as it turned out":

> The most important innovation in cycling, as it turned out, was one introduced for the benefit of women cyclists, who hesitated, in their voluminous skirts, to rise so high above the earth.[13]

The words "as it turned out" can be dropped from that sentence and replaced with ellipsis points. The comma after "cycling" is omitted.

```
The most important innovation in cycling . . . was

one introduced for the benefit of women, who

hesitated, in their voluminous skirts, to rise so

high above the earth.
```

If the comma after "cycling" is retained, it should be kept in the same place as it was in the original and not placed after the ellipsis points:

```
The most important innovation in cycling, . . .

was one introduced for the benefit of women, who

hesitated, in their voluminous skirts, to rise so

high above the earth.
```

**6.5.3. Ellipsis points to replace a sentence or sentences.** When omitting a sentence or longer passage, retain the ending punctuation of the previous sentence and place three ellipsis points after the ending punctuation. This passage will serve as a starting point:

> Foreign travelers had frequently commented on the sallow and unhealthy appearance of American males, notably businessmen and those who earned their living by sedentary pursuits. American "nerves" were, it was generally agreed, deplorable. Americans smoked like chimneys and drank like fish.[14]

Notice the use of the period and ellipsis points after "pursuits" in the following example. No space appears between "pursuits" and the period, as is standard with ending punctuation. A single space appears between the period and the first ellipsis point and between each ellipsis point. Two spaces appear between the final ellipsis point and the resumption of text.

```
Foreign travelers had frequently commented on the

sallow and unhealthy appearance of American males,

notably businessmen and those who earned their

living by sedentary pursuits. . . . Americans

smoked like chimneys and drank like fish.
```

If you ended the first sentence after "males," you would not retain the comma that appears there. Use a period and three points.

```
Foreign travelers had frequently commented on the

sallow and unhealthy appearance of American

males. . . .  American "nerves" were, it was

generally agreed, deplorable.
```

**6.5.4. Ellipsis points in place of lines of poetry.** The omission of a line or several consecutive lines of poetry is shown by a line of ellipsis points approximately the length of the line above it.

```
Ask me no more where Jove bestows,

. . . . . . . . . . . . . . . . . . . . . . . . . . . . . .

For in your beauty's orient deep

These flowers, as in their causes, sleep.[15]
```

**6.5.5. Ellipsis points not needed.** Ellipsis points are not needed at the beginning or end of a quoted passage. That statement holds true whether the quoted passage is a sentence fragment, a complete sentence, or more, and whether the quotation is run in or block indented. The rationale is that unless you are quoting the first or last sentence of a work, something comes before and something follows what is quoted, and readers are well aware of that fact.

EXCEPTION: Ending ellipsis points should be used when the thought of the passage is incomplete:

```
If women had wives to keep house for them, to stay
home with vomiting children, to get the car fixed,
fight with the painters. . . .16
```

### 6.5.6. Capitalization following ellipsis points. A lowercase letter in the original may be changed to a capital letter when quoted if it indicates that a new sentence is beginning.

This principle can be demonstrated by using the following passage, in its entirety, from Daniel J. Boorstin's *The Discoverers*:

> He did not make his living by astronomy or by any application of astronomy. By our standards, at least, he was wonderfully versatile, which put him in the mainstream of the High Renaissance.[17]

The word *he* in the last sentence may be capitalized when the passage is quoted thus:

```
He did not make his living by astronomy or by any
application of astronomy. . . . He was
wonderfully versatile, which put him in the
mainstream of the High Renaissance.
```

# CHAPTER 7

# GRAPHICS

As used here, the word *graphics* includes tables and charts. This definition excludes more complicated forms such as illustrations and photographs.

Writers of term papers produce or obtain graphics by three methods. Some have the talent to use artists' materials and hand-draw the graphics. Others use computers, and others copy the graphic from an article or book.

Because of the variety of techniques involved, this chapter cannot offer guidelines on how to draw graphics. Instead, the advice here deals with the fundamental aspects of choosing those graphics that will help readers understand what you are writing about.

## 7.1. Text or Graphics—Which Will It Be?

A graphic aid can be an efficient way of showing a large amount of data that would be hard to read in text. Consider the following paragraph, which presents a relatively small set of numbers.

The use of high technology in college classrooms increased dramatically in the early 1980s. As an example, in 1982 seventeen percent of first-year college students took a computer-assisted course. That number increased to twenty-six percent in 1983 and to forty percent in 1984. In 1982 twenty-seven percent of first-year college students wrote a computer program. That figure increased to thirty-eight percent in 1983 and to fifty-one percent in 1984.[1]

Compare that paragraph to table 7a, which makes the numbers more easily seen.

Table 7a

Computer Uses by First-year College Students

1982 to 1984

| Characteristic | Percent of first-year college students | | |
|---|---|---|---|
| | 1982 | 1983 | 1984 |
| Taken a computer-assisted course | 17 | 26 | 40 |
| Written a computer program | 27 | 38 | 51 |

Another way to show the same set of figures is to use a chart. A bar chart, such as in figure 7a, allows for a quick comparison of the numbers. However, the chart does not show the percentages as precisely as the table does.

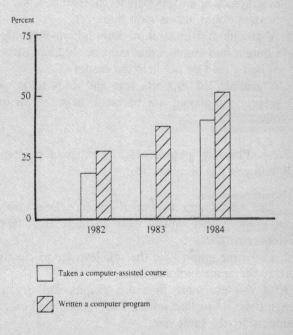

Figure 7a
Computer Uses by First-year College Students,
1982 to 1984

☐ Taken a computer-assisted course

▨ Written a computer program

Choosing the right method is often a matter of trial and error. If you are considering the use of graphics, you will have to experiment with different layouts of tables and charts to see which does the job best.

## 7.2. General Principles for Using Graphics

To use graphic aids, you must first be aware of these cautions:

- For many readers, graphics are Greek. Looking at graphics is an unwelcome chore that a lot of readers would just as soon skip over.
- A graphic aid must show information instantly. Complicated graphics that must be studied instead of being read do not help the reader.
- A graphic aid supports text and adds to it. A graphic aid should not be made to stand on its own.

**7.2.1. Planning graphic aids.** This list of pointers will help you plan graphic aids:

1. Use a minimum number of graphics. Select only those graphics that explain items in the text or help readers remember.
2. Make the graphic aid the smallest size to clearly portray the desired information.
3. If you use more than one graphic aid, try to design them all so that words, lines, scales, and other elements are the same size.
4. Make the terms in the graphic aids consistent with terms used in the text.
5. Treat graphics the same as words: Use few and keep them simple.

**7.2.2. Integrating graphics into text.** A graphic aid should be put as close as possible to where it is first mentioned in the text. To introduce a graphic aid, mention it in these terms:

1. Tell the reader that the graphic aid exists. Mention the aid early so that the reader can refer to it while reading.

2. Refer to the graphic aid by number: "Please see figure 3." Do not refer to "the table below" or "the chart on the next page." By the time your paper has gone through several drafts, the table may not be below, and the chart may not be on the next page. Graphics are numbered in sequence throughout the paper.

3. Comment on the major points of the graphic. Give the reader some help in understanding what the graphic is about.

**7.2.3. Computer-related problems.** The graphic you see on a computer screen sometimes does not look sharp when printed, and the problem often can be traced to the printer and the quality of the paper used. Characters and lines come out with jagged edges, called *jaggies*, the ink on some letters fills in, and an *S* turns into a *5*.

The cures are to change paper or printer, and not to burden the reader with these kinds of problems.

**7.2.4. Citing sources.** The source of information in a graphic may be placed in a note with the graphic or at the end of the paper.

CROSS-REFERENCE: Titles of graphics are written according to the instructions in section 4.5.2.

## 7.3. Tables to Show Numbers

Tables are good for showing numbers. Moreover, a table has the added advantage that it can be prepared on a typewriter. No special artists' equipment is needed.

A table has at least two columns, a title, and a number. The headings at the top of the columns are called *boxheads*; the far left column is known as the *stub*.

**7.3.1. Stub arrangement.** The listing in the stub should give the reader a pattern to follow. Common patterns are alphabetical, chronological, or by classifications. Items in the stub are usually not numbered.

**7.3.2. Capitalization.** Stub, column, and boxhead entries are capitalized in sentence style; that is, only the first word and proper nouns are capitalized.

**7.3.3. Alignment.** Figures are aligned on the right. Symbols such as commas, decimal points, and dollar, percent, plus, and minus signs are aligned vertically. Numbers are rounded off to no more than two decimal places.

**7.3.4. Abbreviations and devices.** Omit periods and use standard abbreviations and symbols. Unusual or new devices can be explained in a note. Avoid using ditto marks.

**7.3.5. Rules (lines).** The lines between elements are called *rules*. Horizontal rules are easy to do on a typewriter, but vertical rules take more time and effort. A way to resolve this problem is to rule tables only if spacing will not provide enough separation.

**7.3.6. Spacing.** Double-space tables throughout.

For reference, see table 7a, which was prepared according to these guidelines.

## 7.4. Charts to Show Relationships

**7.4.1. Bar charts.** Bar (column) charts enable readers to see relationships. The bars can be arranged horizontally or vertically. Figure 7b uses vertical bars to show the number of speakers of the three principal languages of the world.

Figure 7b
Three Principal Languages of the World, 1985[2]

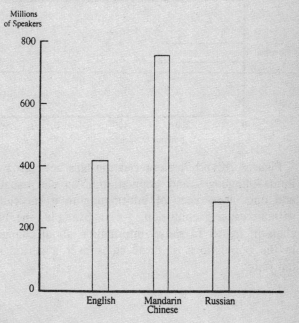

This same information is shown with horizontal bars in figure 7c.

Figure 7c
Three Principal Languages of the World, 1985

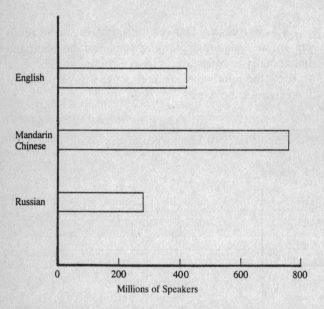

Millions of Speakers

Figures 7b and 7c show relationships between two items—languages and population. You can usually add one more piece of information to a bar chart without causing confusion. As an example, the bar chart in figure 7d shows information about changes in the populations of three cities over a period of ten years.

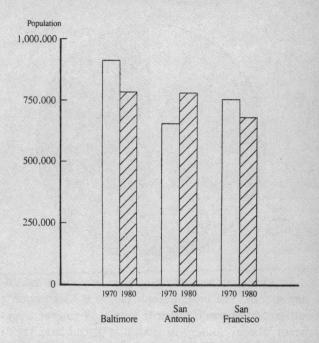

Figure 7d
Population Changes in Baltimore, San Antonio,
and San Francisco, 1970 to 1980[3]

**7.4.2. Pie charts.** Percentages can be compared in a pie chart, as shown in figure 7e.

Figure 7e
Percentage of Popular Vote, 1980 Presidential Election[4]

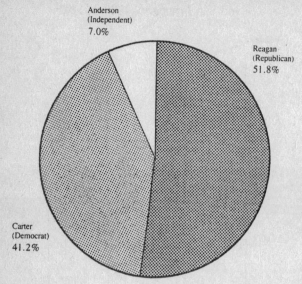

Anderson
(Independent)
7.0%

Reagan
(Republican)
51.8%

Carter
(Democrat)
41.2%

In a pie chart sectors are arranged clockwise according to size. The largest sector begins at "high noon"; progressively smaller sectors follow. Whenever a segment labeled "other" is used, it is placed last. Try to limit the number of segments to five.

For constructing a pie chart, some percentage values of a circle are:

| 360 | degrees | = | 100 | percent |
|-----|---------|---|-----|---------|
| 180 | degrees | = | 50  | percent |
| 90  | degrees | = | 25  | percent |
| 36  | degrees | = | 10  | percent |
| 18  | degrees | = | 5   | percent |
| 3.6 | degrees | = | 1   | percent |

## 7.5. Charts to Show Trends

Line charts enable readers to see trends. A line chart may carry one or more lines. If too many lines are carried, the chart will be cluttered and will confuse the reader.

**7.5.1. Chart with a single line.** Figure 7f shows a line chart with a single line. The trend depicted is that of the apparent decline in the number of males entering college in the United States. The numbers given represent percentage of total enrollment.

Figure 7f
Percentage, of Total Enrollment, of Males
Entering College in the United States, 1966 to 1984[5]

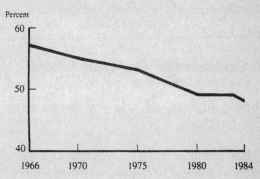

**7.5.2. Chart with two lines.** In this case, the single line of figure 7f tells only part of the story. The missing part is the increase in the number of females attending. That increase can be shown by adding another line, in this case a broken line. Both lines are labeled to help readers.

Figure 7g
Percentage of Males and Females Entering
College in the United States, 1966 to 1984[6]

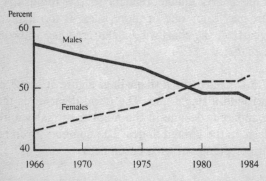

Line charts may contain more than two lines provided great care is taken to keep the lines separate;
label the lines, and use dots, dashes, or broken lines
so that the lines will obviously look different.

## 7.6. Guidelines for Designing Charts

These guidelines will help you design better bar,
line, or pie charts.

1. Bar and line charts are usually laid out as ob-
longs. Scales of 4:3 or 7:4 are common. As an example, a chart can be laid out with a horizontal scale of
seven inches and a vertical scale of four. When the
chart is finished, it can be photographically reduced to
take up less of the page. Many photocopy machines
have reduction features.

2. The title has the largest lettering. The title and

the figure number usually appear above the chart. An exception can be made when better visual balance is achieved by placing the title and number in a corner of the chart.

3. Label curves or bars on the chart, and place labels horizontally. Boxing of labels should be avoided; it's extra work and a distraction for the reader. When a key is necessary, it should be placed where it will balance other elements of the chart. Notes containing explanations or source citations are placed below the chart.

4. On line and bar charts, many values have zero as a reference. When zero is the reference, show it; to do otherwise is to cheat the reader. An exception can be made for values such as the Gross National Product, which never was at zero. Line charts without zero references are shown in figures 7f and 7g.

5. Avoid extreme contrasts of diagonal and straight lines; otherwise, optical illusions may result.

# CHAPTER 8

## CITING SOURCES

This chapter shows four methods of citing sources. The four are bibliographies, endnotes, parenthetical citations, and citations to a numbered reference list. A bibliography is the most general of forms of citation. It shows a list of works consulted but does not give page numbers. Endnotes and other similar forms of citation show page numbers on which material may be found.

## 8.1. Source Citations—General

**8.1.1. Purposes.** You cite sources for two reasons. One is to show readers where you obtained your material. The other is to offer readers a list of references should they want to read more about the subject.

Your list of sources contains the facts of publication for the documents that you use. These items vary, depending upon whether the document is an article or a book. The following sections describe how to obtain and use the facts of publication.

**8.1.2. Obtaining the facts of publication for a book.** To obtain the facts of publication for a book, check the title page and the back of the title page. In some publications, such as documents produced by governmental organizations, some of the facts of publication are also found on the last pages of the work.

For a book, the facts of publication are:

Name or names of the author(s), editor(s), compiler(s), translator(s), or institution responsible for preparing the book.

Full title, including subtitle, if any.

Title of series, if any; number of books in series, if applicable; volume number, if any; edition number, if any.

Place of publication. Place of publication includes, as a minimum, the name of a city and frequently the name of a state, province, or country.

Name of publisher.

Date of publication. The date of publication is found on the *back* of the title page and is the latest copyright date. Do not use the latest printing date. The date you want is introduced with "Copyright" or the symbol ©.

Page numbers. For a bibliography entry, you do not need to copy the number of pages in the book. For notes or in-text references, you will need specific citations to a page or pages in the book.

**8.1.3. Obtaining the facts of publication for an article.** Some of the facts of publication for an article are found on the first page of the article. Other facts of publication are found in the front of the magazine, near the table of contents. There you will find the complete name of the publication together with volume number, issue number, and date of publication.

For an article, the facts of publication are:

Name(s) of the author(s).
Title of the article.
Name of the periodical.
Volume number, if used; issue number, if used.
Date of publication.
Page numbers. For a bibliography, use inclusive pages occupied by the article. For notes or in-text references, use specific citations to a page or pages in the article.

**8.1.4. "Changing" the facts of publication.** To be literal, you cannot change a fact. However, you may make some "changes" to the facts of publication so that you can establish a consistent style. These changes are described in the following subsections.

**8.1.5. Name of author.** Here *author* refers to the individual or organization responsible for writing, editing, compiling, translating, or otherwise preparing the publication.

If more than one name is listed as author, copy the names in sequence, even if the sequence is not in alphabetical order.

Drop any abbreviations of titles such as *M.D.* or *Ph.D.*

**8.1.6. Titles.** In general, underline the title of an entire publication, such as a book or newspaper, and put quotation marks around part of a publication, such as an article or chapter of a book.

CROSS-REFERENCES: The uses of underlining and quotation marks with titles are covered in sections 4.5.3. through 4.5.12. For the capitalization of titles see section 4.5.2.

**8.1.7. Numerals.** Numerals sometimes appear in titles and with any numbers used to identify volume, series, issue, or edition. If a roman numeral appears in the title, leave the numeral in roman. If a roman numeral appears with volume, series, issue, or edition, change the numeral to arabic.

Preface page numbers in roman numerals are to be left in roman.

**8.1.8. Place of publication.** When showing the place of publication, there is no need to give state names with prominent cities such as Boston, Chicago, Los Angeles, or New York.

**8.1.9. Abbreviations for the parts of a document.** Acceptable abbreviations for the parts of a document are:

| PART | ABBREVIATION |
|---|---|
| chapter | chap. |
| edition | ed. |
| Revised edition | Rev. ed. |
| Second edition | 2d ed. |
| editor or editors | ed. or eds. |
| compiler or compilers | comp. or comps. |

| PART | ABBREVIATION |
|------|--------------|
| translator or translators | trans. (singular or plural) |
| page or pages | p. or pp. |
| Volume 4 | Vol. 4 |
| four volumes | 4 vols. |
| Number 3 | No. 3 |
| Part 2 | Pt. 2 |

**8.1.10. Use of page numbers.** For a bibliography entry for a book, no need exists to copy the number of pages in the book. For a bibliography entry for an article, copy the inclusive pages of the article. When writing notes or other in-text references, you will have to copy specific page numbers.

When showing inclusive page numbers, use a hyphen between the page numbers and show all the numbers: 76-69, not 76-9; 101-105, not 101-5.

The abbreviations *p.* and *pp.* are not necessary.

**8.1.11. Missing facts of publication.** When it is not possible to obtain all the facts of publication, abbreviations can be used:

| ITEM | ABBREVIATION |
|------|--------------|
| place of publication not given | n.p. |
| publisher not given | n.p. |
| date of publication not given | n.d. |
| page number(s) not given | n. pag. |

The abbreviation is inserted where the missing fact of publication should appear.

## 8.2. Bibliographies

**8.2.1. Bibliographies—general.** A bibliography is a list of works consulted.

Items are arranged alphabetically, disregarding the articles *a*, *an*, and *the*. A long bibliography may be broken into sections based on topics or type of publications consulted. Within each section, items are listed alphabetically.

In a bibliography, authors' names are reversed, that is, given last name first. Periods separate the major elements of author, title, and publication data. Page numbers are not included for a book but are included for an article.

CROSS-REFERENCE: For the typing of bibliographies, see 9.4.17.

**8.2.2. Bibliography style for a book by one author.** A bibliography entry for a book by one author resembles this example:

```
Brinkley, Allan.  Voices of Protest:  Huey Long,
     Father Coughlin, and the Great Depression.
     New York:  Alfred A. Knopf, 1982.
```

**8.2.3. Bibliography style for a book by two authors.** For two authors, commas are used to separate names:

```
Graves, Robert, and Hodge, Alan.  The Reader over
     Your Shoulder:  A Handbook for Writers of
     English Prose.  2d ed.  New York:  Random
     House, 1971.
```

**8.2.4. Bibliography style for a book by three or more authors.** For three or more authors, semicolons are used to separate names:

```
McCrum, Robert; Cran, William; and MacNeil,

    Robert.  The Story of English.  New York:

    Viking Penguin, 1986.
```

When there are more than three authors, you could include the names of all the authors, space permitting. What is more commonly done is to use just the first author's name and the expression *and others* or *et al.* If you use *et al.*, it is not underlined, and a period is used after *al.* but not after *et.*

```
Bradock, Richard, and others.  Research in Written

    Composition.  Urbana, Ill.:  National Council

    of Teachers of English, 1963.
```

**8.2.5. Bibliography style for a book by an organization.** When an organization is the writer of a document, the bibliographic style is the same as for a document by a single author.

```
U.S. Department of Commerce.  Pocket Data Book

    USA 1976.  Washington, D.C.:  U.S. Government

    Printing Office, November 1976.
```

**8.2.6. Bibliography style for a book by an author with a pen name.** Use the pen name of an author when that is what the title page shows. No need exists to supply the real name, because library catalogs provide plenty of cross-references. Punctuation follows the style for a book by one author (see section 8.2.2).

**8.2.7. Bibliography style for a book with the author's name not given.** If the author's name is known but not given on the title page, the bibliography entry shows the name in brackets. Note that the period goes inside the brackets.

```
[Harrington, Charles.]  The Deacon's Surprise,
    and Other Follies.  London, 1733.
```

If the name of the author involves guesswork, a question mark is placed inside the brackets:

```
[Harrington, Charles?]  The Deacon's Surprise,
    and Other Follies.  London, 1733.
```

If the author's name (or the name of the editor, compiler, or translator) is neither given nor ascertainable, begin the bibliography entry with the title of the work. Do not use *anon.* or *anonymous.*

```
Air Pollution Primer.  New York:  National
    Tuberculosis and Respiratory Disease
    Association, 1971.
```

**8.2.8. Bibliography style for a book with editor, compiler, or translator in place of author.** A bibliography item begins with the name of a book's editor, compiler, or translator when one of these is listed on the title page and no author's name is given. *Editor* or other term is abbreviated and placed after the name:

```
DeVoto, Bernard, ed.  Mark Twain: Letters from
     the Earth.  New York:  Harper & Row, 1962.


Mandelbaum, Allen, trans.  The Aeneid of Virgil.
     New York:  Bantam Books, 1971.


Bullock, Alan, and Stallybrass, Oliver, eds.  The
     Harper Dictionary of Modern Thought.  New
     York:  Harper & Row, 1977.
```

**8.2.9. Bibliography style for a book with editor, compiler, or translator in addition to author.** When an author's name appears on the title page together with the name of an editor, compiler, or translator, begin the bibliography entry with the author's name. Place the name of the editor, compiler, or translator after the title:

```
Twain, Mark.  Adventures of Huckleberry Finn.
     Edited by Henry Nash Smith.  Boston:
     Houghton Mifflin Co., 1958.
```

**8.2.10. Bibliography style for a book edition, series, or volume.** The edition, series, or volume is placed after the book's title:

Himstreet, William C., and Baty, Wayne Murlin.
    Business Communications: Principles and
    Methods. 7th ed. Boston: Kent Publishing
    Company, 1984.


Mencken, H. L. The American Language: An Inquiry
    into the Development of English in the United
    States. 4th ed., corrected, enlarged, and
    rewritten. New York: Alfred A. Knopf, 1936.


Mencken, H. L. The American Language: An Inquiry
    into the Development of English in the United
    States. Supplement 1. New York: Alfred A.
    Knopf, 1945.


Handbook on California's Natural Resources.
    Vol. 2, Sacramento, Calif.: Resources Agency
    of California, 1970.


Churchill, Winston E. The Second World War. 6
    vols. Boston: Houghton Mifflin Co., 1948.


Tierney, Brian, and others, eds. The Origins of
    Modern Imperialism--Ideological or Economic?
    Random House Historical Issues Series,
    No. 19. New York: Random House, Inc., 1967.

**8.2.11. Bibliography style for a book in a reprinted edition.** When writing an entry for a reprinted edition of a book, data on the reprinting publisher are given after data on the original publisher:

```
Bierce, Ambrose.  The Devil's Dictionary.  Neale

    Publishing Co., 1911.  Reprint.  New York:

    Dover Publications, Inc., 1958.
```

**8.2.12. Bibliography style for an unpublished work.** An unpublished work such as a thesis, manuscript, or book in draft is treated the same as a published book but with two exceptions. The title is placed in quotation marks and is not underlined, and the word *thesis* or a similar term is used to label the work:

```
Willoughby, Thomas H.  "Student Evaluation of

    California State Service."  M.A. thesis.

    Sacramento, Cal.:  California State

    University, Sacramento, 1959.
```

**8.2.13. Bibliography style for articles.** The instructions for listing articles in a bibliography pertain to articles, essays, or stories in a periodical.

When listing articles, list authors' names in the same manner that you would list authors' names for books. Then give title of the article in quotation marks, title of the periodical underlined, volume number and issue number and date, and the inclusive pages that the article appeared on.

The abbreviations *Vol.*, *No.*, and *p.* or *pp.* will not be necessary if these references are handled as shown here:

- When you know only the volume numbers, simply show it as an arabic number—16.
- When you know volume and issue number, separate the two with a colon—16:4.
- When adding page numbers, set them off with a comma—16:4, 27-31.
- The date of publication is placed in parentheses after the volume and issue—16:4 (April 1979), 27-31.

```
Lowenthal, Marjorie Fisk, and Chiriboga, David.

    "Transition to the Empty Nest."  Archives of

    General Psychiatry.  26 (January 1972), 8-14.


"Word Processing:  How Will It Shape the Student

    as a Writer?"  Classroom Computer News

    (November/December 1982), 24-27, 74-76.


Martin, F.; Roberts, K.; and Collins, A.

    "Short-term Memory for Sentences."  Journal

    of Verbal Learning and Verbal Behavior.  7

    (1968), 560-566.


"Two Gun Laws Have No Real Effect."  Newsweek

    (October 4, 1982), 17.


Coburn, Judith.  "The Last Patrol."  Mother Jones.

    12:2 (February/March 1987), 37-45.
```

With newspapers, it is sometimes necessary to give the section number or name with the page number:

```
Clines, Francis X.   "The Mother Tongue Has a
     Movement."  New York Times (June 3, 1984), 8E.


Corwin, Miles.  "A City with Its Own 'Official
     Language.'"  San Francisco Chronicle
     (May 19, 1985), Punch, 3.
```

When an article is "continued," give the page that the article starts on and the page or pages on which it continues. A comma separates the pages:

```
Parvel, Miriam.  "Nine Great Myths about Mario
     Cuomo," Mother Jones.  12:2 (February/March
     1987), 27-33, 49.
```

**8.2.14. Bibliography style for a work cited in another work.** On occasion you will want to refer to a work cited in another work, such as an article mentioned in another article or book. Because readers might wish to find either work, you should give as much information as you can about both.

```
Walpole, Jane R.  "Why Must the Passive Be
     Damned?"  College Composition and
     Communication.  30:3 (October 1979), 251.  In
     Bush, Don.  "The Passive Voice Should Be
     Avoided--Sometimes."  Technical Communication,
     28:1 (First Quarter 1981), 19-20, 22.
```

```
Ringer, Robert J.  "How People Get the Things They
     Want."  Chapter 3 in Restoring the American
     Dream.  New York:  Fawcett Crest Books, 1979.
     71-120.
```

**8.2.15. Bibliography style for government documents.**
When a government document is produced by an
agency, follow the style shown for a book by an organization. If the author(s) name or names are known,
use the style appropriate to the number of names.

**8.2.16. Bibliography style for a computer software
program.** When writing a bibliography entry for a
computer software program, include the writer of the
program, if known; the title of the program underlined; the label *Computer software* neither underlined
nor enclosed in quotation marks; the distributor; and
the year of publication. Separate items with periods,
but place a comma between distributor and year of
publication.

At the end of the entry add any other pertinent
information—for example, the computer for which
the software was designed, the number of units
of memory, and the form of the program. Separate
these items with commas and end the entry with a
period:

```
Peterson, David.  Mail Games.  Computer software.
     Creative Software, 1981.  Atari 400/800,
     32KB, disk.
```

When the name of the software writer is not known,
begin with the title of the program:

Connections.  Computer software.  Krell Software,

    1982.

**8.2.17. Bibliography style for an on-line information source.** Material from an on-line (computer) information source such as DIALOG is treated like printed material, but with a reference to the source at the end of the entry. This reference should include the name of the source and identifying numbers provided by the source:

Howard, R. K.  "Chess Games and the Early

    Adolescent."  Elementary Education.  27:6

    (June 1983), 88-93.  DIALOG file 123,

    item 177000 061823.

**8.2.18. Bibliography style for legal references.** If you must have any references to legal documents, consult the Harvard Law Review Association's *Uniform System of Citation*. Otherwise do not use underlining or quotation marks with the titles of laws, acts, or similar documents, and use only familiar abbreviations:

U.S. Const. Art. 1, sec. 1.


Section 14955 of the California Government Code.


When referring to the United States Code, the title number precedes the code:

                12 U.S.C.

Court cases are italicized:

Johnson v. Leatherby

**8.2.19. Bibliography style for a film.** Films, video-tapes, slide programs, and other audiovisual materials can be identified by title, writer, producer, director, stars, or production studio. All of that information isn't necessary, but enough should be provided so that the reader can find the wanted item.

Managing Your Time More Effectively.  Sacramento,

   Calif.:  Holrod Visuals, 1987.  Slides.


Marx Brothers.  Animal Crackers.  1930.


Scott, Tony, director.  Top Gun.  Paramount, 1986.

**8.2.20. Bibliography style for a lecture.** A lecture or paper read at a meeting has its title placed in quotation marks. Other language identifies the speaker and the event.

Ferraro, Geraldine A.  "Who Will Fight for the

   Worth of Women's Work."  Speech delivered

   at the annual meeting of the National

   Association of Women Judges.  New York.

   October 9, 1982.


Tepley, Paul T.  "Liability for Technical

   Communication Professionals as Developed in

   the Courts."  Paper presented at the 34th

   International Technical Communications

   Conference.  Denver, Colorado.  May 10, 1987.

**8.2.21. Bibliography style for an interview or a conversation.** When citing an interview or a conversation in a bibliography, include the name of the other person, the word *author* (as a reference to yourself), and the place and date.

Jones, Marcy.  Interview with the author.

    Manhattan, Kansas.  April 17, 1987.

**8.2.22. Bibliography style for a letter.** When citing a letter or a memo in a bibliography, include the name of the other person, the word *author* as a reference to yourself, and the date of the correspondence.

Jones, Marcy.  Letter to the author.  April 22,

    1987.

**8.2.23. Bibliography style for a musical piece.** If you are citing a printed musical score, use quotation marks around the title of a short piece or any part of a longer piece, and underline the title of a long work or a complete work containing smaller parts.

Debussy, Claude.  "La plus que lente."  Paris,

    France:  Editions Durand, 1910.


Grieg, Edvard.  <u>Concerto for Piano</u>, Op. 16.

    New York:  G. Schirmer, 1920.

If you are citing a recording, identify it as a disc, cassette, phonorecord, or tape.

Chopin, Frédéric.  "Etude."  Op. 10, No. 8.

    Tamás Vásáry, pianist.  Polydor International

    GmbH 3335 266.  Cassette.

**8.2.24. Repeated bibliography items.** When several works by the same author are listed in sequence, you may repeat the author's name. An alternative, which will require the reader to glance back up the page, is to list the author's name at the first entry only and from then on use a line of five hyphens in place of the author's name. Alphabetical arrangement is by title, and a period follows the line of hyphens:

```
Catton, Bruce.  Grant Takes Command.  Boston:

     Little, Brown and Co., 1969.


-----.  This Hallowed Ground:  The Story of the

     Union Side of the Civil War.  Garden City,

     N.Y.:  Doubleday & Company, Inc., 1956.
```

## 8.3. Notes (Footnotes, Endnotes)

**8.3.1. Notes—general.** Notes such as those described here are called *footnotes* when they are placed at the bottom of the page. When placed at the end of the paper, they are called *endnotes*. The term used here is the more general one, *notes*.

Term papers should be prepared with endnotes. Footnotes are rarely used, except for theses, dissertations, and some scholarly journals. If you should be required to use footnotes, follow these instructions: (1) Drop down four spaces from the last line of text on the page; (2) type a solid, horizontal line fifteen spaces long beginning at the left margin; (3) immediately below the line type each note single-spaced, with double-spacing between notes; (4) follow the style of writing and typing notes as shown in sections 8.3.3 through 8.3.24 and 9.4.18 through 9.4.20; and (5) make sure the last line of a note does not fall below the bottom margin.

If it is necessary to continue a footnote to the next page, separate the continued note from text with quadruple spacing and a fifteen-space-long line. Footnotes for the new page immediately follow the note continued from the previous page.

**8.3.2. Showing a note in text.** A note is called to the reader's attention by use of a number typed slightly above the line (a superior number or superscript).[1] Notes are numbered consecutively throughout the paper. The superior number refers to a page or pages in the publication listed in the endnotes.

Superior numbers follow all punctuation except the dash:

```
"This is all that was offered."[1]


(For the most recent trend, see the annual
supplement.)[2]


Bernstein says so[3]--as do many others.
```

When more than one superior number must be used, place a comma between each number so that [1,2] will not be misread as something else. [12]

**8.3.3. Note style.** In a note, the author's name is given first name first. Place and date of publication and name of publisher are placed in parentheses. Page numbers identify the location of material; the abbreviations *p.* and *pp.* are not necessary. A period ends each note.

CROSS-REFERENCE: For the typing of endnotes, see section 9.4.17.

**8.3.4. When to use a note.** You use a note and its superior number with three types of information:

- Immediately after a quotation
- Immediately after a specific element such as a statistic or a startling fact
- At the end of a paragraph or section on a major occurrence or concept

Do not use a note with a well-known event like Columbus's discovery of America.

**8.3.5. Note for a book by one author.** Note style for a book by one author follows this example:

1.  J. B. Bury, The Idea of Progress: An Inquiry
    into Its Origin and Growth (New York:
    Macmillan, 1932), 111-121.

**8.3.6. Note for a book by two authors.** For a book by two authors, the authors' names are joined by *and*:

2.  Robert Graves and Alan Hodge, The Reader Over
    Your Shoulder: A Handbook for Writers of
    English Prose, 2d ed. (New York: Random
    House, 1971), 41.

**8.3.7. Note for a book by three or more authors.** In a note for a book by three or more authors, commas separate names:

3. Robert McCrum, William Cran, and Robert
   MacNeil, The Story of English (New York:
   Viking Penguin, 1986), 115-116.

When there are more than three authors, it is permissible to shorten the reference by using *and others* or *et al.*:

4. Richard Bradock and others, Research in
   Written Composition (Urbana, Ill.: National
   Council of Teachers of English, 1963), 88-91.

**8.3.8. Note for a book by an organization.** For a book by an organization, the name of the organization appears as the name of the author:

5. Office of Technology Assessment. The Effects
   of Nuclear War (Washington, D.C.: U.S.
   Government Printing Office, 1979), 9-13.

**8.3.9. Note for a book by an author with a pen name.** Use the author's pen name if that is what the title page shows, and follow the style for a note by a single author (see section 8.3.5).

**8.3.10. Note for a book with author's name not given.** If the author's name is known but not given on the title page, the note shows the name in brackets.

The comma after the name is placed outside the brackets:

6.  [Charles Harrington], The Deacon's Surprise, and Other Follies (London 1783), 6-8.

If the author's name involves guesswork, a question mark is placed inside the brackets:

7.  [Charles Harrington?], The Deacon's Surprise, and Other Follies (London 1783), 6-8.

If the author's name (or the name of the editor, compiler, or translator) is neither given nor ascertainable, begin the entry with the title of the work. Do not use *anon.* or *anonymous*:

8.  Environmental Quality (Washington, D.C.; U.S. Government Printing Office, 1978), 435.

**8.3.11. Note for a book with editor, compiler, or translator in place of author.** A note begins with the name of the book's editor, compiler, or translator when one of these is listed on the title page and no author's name is given. A comma separates the name from *ed.* (*eds.*), *comp.* (*comps.*), or *trans.*:

9.  Allen Mandelbaum, trans., The Aeneid of Virgil (New York:  Bantam Books, 1971), 7-8.

10.  Charles R. Cooper and Lee Odell, eds., Research on Composing:  Points of Departure (Urbana, Ill.:  National Council of Teachers of English, 1978), 99-101.

**8.3.12. Note for a book with editor, compiler, or translator in addition to author.** Sometimes an author's name appears on the title page together with the name of an editor, compiler, or translator. In that case, the note begins with the author's name, and the editor's, compiler's, or translator's name appears after the title. The abbreviations are *ed.* ("edited by"), *comp.* ("compiled by"), and *trans.* ("translated by"). Accordingly, no plural form such as *eds.* is used.

11. Mark Twain, Adventures of Huckleberry Finn, ed. Henry Nash Smith (Boston: Houghton Mifflin Co., 1958), vii.

**8.3.13. Note for a book edition, series, or volume.** Edition, series, or volume identification is placed after the book's title.

12. William C. Himstreet and Wayne Murlin Baty, Business Communications: Principles and Methods, 7th ed. (Boston: Kent Publishing Company, 1984), 197-213.

13. H. L. Mencken, The American Language: An Inquiry into the Development of English in the United States, 4th ed., corrected, enlarged, and rewritten (New York: Alfred A. Knopf, 1936), viii.

14. H. L. Mencken, The American Language: An Inquiry into the Development of English in the United States, supplement 1 (New York: Alfred A. Knopf, 1945), ix-xi.

15.  <u>Handbook on California's Natural Resources</u>,
     vol. 2 (Sacramento, Calif.:  Resources
     Agency of California, 1970), 51.

16.  Brian Tierney and others, eds., <u>The Origins</u>
     <u>of Modern Imperialism--Ideological or</u>
     <u>Economic?</u>  Random House Historical Issues
     Series, No. 19 (New York:  Random House,
     Inc., 1967), 39-43.

**8.3.14. Note for a book in a reprint edition.** When
writing a note for a reprinted edition of a book, data
on the reprinting publisher are given after data on the
original publisher:

17.  Ambrose Bierce, <u>The Devil's Dictionary</u>
     (Neale Publishing Co., 1911; reprint, New
     York:  Dover Publications, Inc., 1958), 25.

**8.3.15. Note for a major reference work.** A note
that cites a well-known reference work need not include the publisher's name and date and place of publication. The edition, if not the first, must be specified.
In addition, references to an alphabetically organized
work are not to page number but to the title of the entry:

18.  <u>Webster's New International Dictionary</u>,
     2d ed., "quake."

19.  <u>Who's Who in America</u>, 40th ed., "Flesch,
     Rudolf."

**8.3.16. Note for a biblical reference.** References to
the Bible should include book, chapter, and verse. A

colon or a period may be used between chapter and verse. Book titles may be abbreviated; underlining and quotation marks are not used.

20.  Gen. 7:8-11

21.  2 Cor. 8.4

**8.3.17. Note for an unpublished work.** A thesis, dissertation, or book in draft is an unpublished work. Its title is placed in quotation marks, not underlined, and it is identified with the word *thesis* or something similar:

22.  Thomas H. Willoughby, "Student Evaluation of California State Service," M.A. thesis (Sacramento, Calif.: California State University, Sacramento, 1959), 77.

**8.3.18. Note for an article.** When writing notes for articles, list authors' names in the same manner that you would when writing a note for a book. Then give the title of the article in quotation marks, the title of the periodical underlined, volume number or date of publication or both, and the specific page reference:

23.  Isaac Asimov, "In the Game of Energy and Thermodynamics You Can't Break Even," Smithsonian (August 1970), 9.

24.  Stanley Angrist and Loren Hepler, "Demons, Poetry, and Life: A Thermodynamic View," Texas Quarterly 10 (September 1967), 27.

25.  "Two Gun Laws Have No Real Effect," Newsweek (October 4, 1982), 17.

When citing newspapers it is sometimes necessary to give the section number or name; those go with the page number:

26.   Francis X. Clines, "The Mother Tongue Has a
      Movement," New York Times (June 3, 1984),
      8E.

27.   Miles Corwin, "A City with Its Own 'Official
      Language,'" San Francisco Chronicle
      (May 19, 1985), Punch, 3.

**8.3.19. Note for a work cited in another work.** A note for a reference to a work found in another work should follow this style:

28.   Jean Houston, "Prometheus Rebound:  An
      Inquiry into Technological Growth and
      Psychological Change," in Alternatives to
      Growth I, Dennis Meadows, ed. (Cambridge,
      Mass.:  Ballinger, 1977), 274.

**8.3.20. Note for an on-line information source.** Material from an on-line (computer) information source is treated like printed material, but with a reference to the source at the end of the entry. This reference should include the name of the source and identifying numbers provided by the source:

29.   R. K. Howard, "Chess Games and the Early
      Adolescent," Elementary Education, 27:6
      (June 1983), 91.  DIALOG file 123, item
      177000 061823.

**8.3.21. Note for a letter or a message.** Notes for interviews, letters, memos, or telephone calls are handled according to the style shown here. Words such as *letter* or *memo* are lowercased and not underlined or put in quotation marks:

30. Johns to Davis, letter, August 17, 1863.

31. Interview conducted by the author, May 20, 1987.

**8.3.22. Note for poetry or a play.** Notes for poetry and plays do not include page numbers. Instead, the note cites divisions such as act, scene, verse, canto, and line. The divisions are separated by periods, not commas. Arabic numerals may be substituted for roman.

32. Shakespeare, The Tragedy of Macbeth (New York: Washington Square Press, 1959), II. i. 7-11.

**8.3.23. Note style for a film.** Films, videotapes, slide programs, and other audiovisual materials can be identified by title, writer, producer, director, stars, or production studio. All of that information isn't necessary, but enough should be provided so that the reader can find the wanted item.

33. Marx Brothers, Animal Crackers, 1930.

34. Managing Your Time More Effectively (Sacramento, Calif.: Holrod Visuals, 1987), slides.

35. Tony Scott, director, Top Gun (Paramount, 1986).

**8.3.24. Note style for a lecture.** A lecture or paper read at a meeting has its title placed in quotation marks. Other language identifies the speaker and the event.

36.  Paul T. Tepley, "Liability for Technical Communication Professionals as Developed by the Courts," paper presented at the 34th International Technical Communications Conference (Denver, Colorado, May 10, 1987).

37.  Geraldine A. Ferraro, "Who Will Fight for the Worth of Women's Work," speech delivered at the annual meeting of the National Association of Women Judges (New York, October 9, 1982).

**8.3.25. Note style for a musical piece.** If you are writing a note for a printed musical score, use quotation marks around the title of a short piece or any part of a longer piece, and underline the title of a long work or a complete work containing smaller parts.

38.  Claude Debussy, "Là plus que lente" (Paris, France:   Editions Durand, 1910).

39.  Edvard Grieg, <u>Concerto for Piano</u>, Op. 16 (New York:   G. Schirmer, 1920).

If you are writing a note for a recording, identify it as a disc, cassette, phonorecord, or tape.

40.  Frederic Chopin, "Etude," Op. 10, No. 8, Tamás Vásáry, pianist (Polydor International GmbH 3335 266), cassette.

**8.3.26. Full and shortened notes.** The first time a reference is given, a full citation is used. Subsequent citations to the same source should be shortened. Usually all that is necessary is the author's last name, a short title, and the page number. Ellipsis points are not used to show any deleted material. Examples of full and shortened references are:

41. John Herman Randall, The Making of the Modern Mind (Cambridge, Mass.: Houghton Mifflin, 1940), 33.

42. Randall, Modern Mind, 59.

43. Nicholaus Georgescu-Roegen, "The Steady State and Ecological Salvation," Bio Science (April 1977), 269.

44. Georgescu-Roegen, "Ecological Salvation," 268.

The method demonstrated in notes 41 through 44 is contrary to the older method that relies on Latin abbreviations such as *ibid.* ("the same place") or *op. cit.* ("in the work cited").

Use of the older method poses two problems. One, many modern readers do not know Latin well enough to crack the code at first glance. Two, when a short title is not given, as is the case when Latin abbreviations are used, the reader may have to glance back through several lines or even pages of notes to find out just what work is being referred to.

**8.3.27. Combined notes.** When several references are combined in one note, the individual sources are separated by semicolons:

45.   John Herman Randall, <u>The Making of the Modern</u>
      <u>Mind</u> (Cambridge, Mass.:  Houghton Mifflin,
      1950), 33; Francis X. Clines; "The Mother
      Tongue Has a Movement," <u>New York Times</u>
      (June 3, 1984), 8E; and Stanley Angrist and
      Loren Hepler, "Demons, Poetry, and Life:  A
      Thermodynamic View," <u>Texas Quarterly</u>, 10
      (September 1967), 27.

## 8.4. In-text Citations

**8.4.1. In-text citations—general.** You can also cite sources by using *parenthetical references* placed in the text itself and not at the end of the paper. The reference is arranged in the same manner as a note. That is, authors' names are given first name first. There then appear the title of the reference, the facts of publication, and the page number or numbers. Parentheses are placed around all of the preceding items. Brackets, inside the parentheses, enclose place and name of publisher and date of publication.

**8.4.2. Run-in citation.** The following example shows a parenthetical reference following a prose quotation. The reference begins after the closing quotation mark, and the period comes after the closing parenthesis.

"Abstract words such as glory, honor, courage, or
hallow were obscene" (Ernest Hemingway, <u>A Farewell</u>
<u>to Arms</u> [New York:  Charles Scribner's Sons,
1957], 178).

**8.4.3. Block-indented citation.** The next example shows a parenthetical reference following a block-indented quotation. In this usage no period is necessary after the closing parenthesis.

```
Their candles are all out.  Take thee that too.

A heavy summons lies like lead upon me,

And yet I would not sleep.  Merciful powers,

Restrain in me the cursed thoughts that nature

Gives way to in repose!

(Shakespeare, The Tragedy of Macbeth [New York:

Washington Square Press, 1959], II. i. 7-11)
```

**8.4.4. Subsequent citations.** In writing subsequent references, use the author's last name, short title, and page or division number:

```
(Hemingway, Farewell to Arms, 205)

(Shakespeare, Macbeth, IV. i. 80-85)
```

**8.4.5. In-text citations and multiple ending punctuation.** In some cases an exclamation mark or a question mark ends the quotation. That mark must be retained, and the ending punctuation becomes as shown:

```
"Was this a portrait of Alsinger playing with that

old IBM?"  (Tracy Kidder, The Soul of a New

Machine [New York:  Avon Books, 1981], 96).
```

# 8.5. Citations to a Numbered Reference List

**8.5.1. Citations to a numbered reference list—general.**
A numbered reference list is nothing more than a bibliography in which the items are numbered. The numbers are used in the text to identify specific sources. Endnotes or footnotes are not used, because this method combines notes and bibliography.

**8.5.2. Constructing a numbered reference list.** To construct a numbered reference list, follow these steps:

1. Arrange your bibliography cards in alphabetical order.
2. When writing the bibliography, number each item in sequence, beginning with 1.

A numbered reference list will look like this short example:

1. Bowers, Claude G. <u>The Tragic Era: The Revolution after Lincoln</u>. Cambridge, Massachusetts: Houghton, Mifflin Company, 1957.

2. Commager, Henry Steele. <u>Documents of American History</u>. Vol. 2. New York: Appleton-Century-Crofts, 1958.

3. Dorf, Philip. <u>The Constitution of the United States</u>. New York: Oxford Book Company, 1950.

4. Rossiter, Clinton. <u>The American Presidency</u>. New York: New American Library, 1960.

**8.5.3. Using the references.** An in-text citation to a numbered reference list looks like this next example. Parentheses enclose the citation. The first number is the number of the item on the list. The second number refers to the page or pages in that item. In other words, this example refers to page 12 of item 1. The reference follows the closing quotation mark, and a period appears after the reference.

```
A prominent student of the American presidency

has written about this period that "Never has the

presidency meant less than the years with which

we are concerned" (1:12).
```

CROSS-REFERENCE: For more on multiple punctuation marks with in-text citations, see section 8.4.5.

# CHAPTER 9

# COMPLETING THE PAPER

This chapter shows how to put the finishing touches on a term paper. The steps involved are writing headings, revising, typing, and proofreading.

## 9.1. Writing Headings

### 9.1.1. Headings—general. A heading is a signpost that tells readers what is to come.

A short paper of three to five pages can probably do without headings. As papers become longer or cover more topics, you should consider using headings.

### 9.1.2. The need for informative headings. A heading should give readers a good idea of what the next section of the paper is about. Readers will understand your paper better if you use informative headings instead of vague ones.

To write informative headings, use enough words to describe the content that follows. An example of a list of informative headings is this one from a paper in a sociology course:

I. Curiosity About How a Society Hangs Together
II. The Idea of Societal Change
III. The Use of Systematic Scientific Inquiry

Each of those headings uses enough specific words to give readers a good idea of what to expect.

On the other hand, headings like several on the following list are *not* informative.

Introduction
Part I
Part II
Part III
Conclusions
Bibliography

To be certain, readers know what you mean when you write "Introduction," "Conclusions," and "Bibliography." Otherwise, expressions such as "Part I" tell the reader nothing about the content of that part.

In addition, headings such as "Background" or "Purpose" should be avoided. Those words are too vague to give the reader a good idea of what the material is about.

**9.1.3. The need for parallelism.** *Parallelism* means that similar thoughts should be written in similar grammatical form. Headings should be parallel throughout a paper.

The following two headings are parallel. Both are incomplete sentences, a common style of heading:

I. Curiosity about How a Society Hangs Together
II. The Idea of Societal Change

The next two headings are not parallel. The first is a complete sentence, and the second is not.

I. Sociologists Are Curious about How a Society Hangs Together
II. The Idea of Societal Change

**9.1.4. Number of headings.** As a rule of thumb, you can use one heading for every major point in your outline; you may decide to use more.

**9.1.5. Typing the headings.** Type headings according to the styles shown in figure 9a.

Figure 9a
Styles and Levels of Headings

FIRST-LEVEL HEADING

The first-level heading is typed in all capital letters, underlined, and placed against the left margin. Triple-space or quadruple space above and below the heading.

A first-level heading is used for a major portion of the paper. Smaller portions are introduced with a second-level heading.

Second-level heading. A second-level heading is indented five spaces and underlined; the heading starts a paragraph. Capitalize the first letter of the first word and any proper nouns.

If you need more than two levels of headings, you may vary the styles and underlining as shown here:

FIRST-LEVEL HEADING

SECOND-LEVEL HEADING

    Third-level heading.

Note: Never put a heading at the bottom of a
page unless there is at least one typed line
below it.

**9.1.6. The need for restraint.** Writers who have
word processing equipment often use printers that will
provide boldface, italic, and double strike typefaces in
addition to underlining. If that is your situation, practice some restraint. The use of too many different
typefaces on a page clutters up the page and looks
amateurish.

## 9.2. Revising

**9.2.1. Revising—general.** The effective writer is one
who rewrites. And the effective rewriter is one who
follows this basic rule: *Challenge everything on the
page*. The questions can be arranged into four areas:
material, organization, style, and mechanics.

**9.2.2. Material.** Most first drafts do not contain
enough information. Ideas are not fully developed,
and not enough details are provided to inform or
interest the reader. Therefore, two questions that can
be asked in this area are:

- Should more examples and explanations be provided?
- Do the facts need more interpretation?

**9.2.3. Organization.** The final version must be organized to serve the reader. Overall organization can be checked by asking:

- Can readers quickly find important information?
- Are headings necessary?
- Are headings specific and informative?

Internal organization can be checked by attacking each paragraph with the questions:

- Does each paragraph begin with a topic sentence?
- Is each paragraph limited to a single topic?
- Does one paragraph lead logically to the next, and is the connection obvious?
- Are the gaps filled in?

**9.2.4. Style.** Style can be strengthened by asking questions about sentences and words:

- Does any sentence sound clumsy when read aloud?
- Are sentences too long?
- Are sentences too slow in getting to the point?
- Do sentences contain interrupting elements that break up the flow of thought?
- Is the word choice suitable for the reader?
- Is each word used correctly?
- Does the writing contain any special terms that should be put into plain English?
- Are excess words deleted?

**9.2.5. Mechanics.** Mechanics are all the details of capitalization, grammar, punctuation, quotations, spelling, and the use of numerals. Common problems can be resolved by asking:

- Have I used good grammar?
- Is the writing consistent in the way that numerals and capital letters are used?
- Are spelling and punctuation correct?

The questions presented here do not have to be asked in the order given, and you can ask questions of your own. However you go about revising, the important thing is to dig into the writing, challenge it, and make it better.

Finally, keep in mind that over the years technology has given the writer three worthwhile devices—the eraser, the wastepaper basket, and the DELETE key.

## 9.3. The Order of the Parts

This section lists the parts of a term paper in their correct order. Use the list to make sure that your paper has all of its necessary sections. Instructions for typing the parts are given in section 9.4.

**9.3.1. Title page.** A title page is the term paper's front cover.

**9.3.2. Table of contents.** A table of contents should be used in any paper of ten pages or longer. The table of contents is placed after the title page and lists headings and their page numbers.

**9.3.3. Introduction.** The introduction begins on the page after the table of contents. If no table of contents is used, the introduction begins after the title page. The introduction is page 1 of the paper, the page on which text begins.

**9.3.4. Main body.** The main body is the largest part of the paper. In the main body you present the facts and explanations that derive from your research. You develop your analyses and arguments and show how these relate to the subject and purpose of the report.

The words *main body* are not to be used as a heading, because they are not informative.

**9.3.5. The ending.** The ending contains conclusions and is a general summary of the paper.

**9.3.6. Source citations.** If you did not cite sources in the text, your source citations will be placed at the end of the paper. There source citations will be endnotes, a bibliography, or both. The bibliography may appear before the endnotes or vice versa; the order is not critical.

If you wish to impose some order on the arrangement of this part of the paper, follow this rule: If your list of endnotes is longer than the bibliography, place the endnotes before the bibliography. If the bibliography is the longer of the two, place it before the endnotes.

**9.3.7. An outline.** Some instructors require that an outline be submitted with the paper. Check with your instructor for proper placement of the outline.

## 9.4. Typing the Final Product

**9.4.1. Typing—general.** The qualities of diligent research and painstaking writing will easily show through if your paper is neatly typed. Moreover, instructors would rather read typewritten papers than handwritten ones. Therefore, you should turn in a typewritten paper even if your instructor allows handwritten ones.

You may type the paper yourself, prepare it on a word processor, or have someone else do these things for you. Regardless of who does what, the paper's author bears the ultimate responsibility for turning in a neat, legible paper.

Whether you write or type the final version, certain general principles apply:

- Write or type on one side of the page. Do not place any information on the backs of pages.
- The paper is typed double-spaced. The words *double-spaced* or *double-spacing* mean that you write or type on every other line.
- Keep a copy in case the one you turn in is lost. The kept copy may be carbon or a photocopy. Check with your instructor to see if a photocopy may be turned in instead of an original.

In addition, you will find it helpful to refer to the sample paper in the appendix. That paper follows the style described here.

**9.4.2. Paper selection for typing.** Use white, $8\frac{1}{2} \times 11$ paper. Do not use colored paper. Colored paper is distracting, and it may not photocopy well.

Type the original on good-quality bond paper. The ideal paper has a dull rather than a glossy finish. Do not use crinkly or onionskin paper for the original. It is so thin that the reader looking at one page can see the words on the page behind it.

Paper is classified according to its weight, and stationers use the word *weight* in a technical sense. As far as the writer of a term paper is concerned, paper of twenty-pound weight is acceptable for typing the original. Sixteen-pound paper also is acceptable.

Do not turn in any work typed on erasable paper, which smudges easily. If you prefer to type on erasable paper, then turn in a photocopy.

The carbon copy may be typed on thin paper. Carbon paper should be black and have a hard (nongreasy) finish.

**9.4.3. The typewriter.** Before starting to make the final copy, check your typewriter. Use a fresh ribbon, and *use black*. Colored inks are annoying, and some, especially blue, do not photocopy well or at all. Clean the keys with a brush and a pin. You don't want letters such as *a, e, o, b,* and *d* to fill in with ink.

You should be using a machine with a regular type, either pica or elite. Script and other unusual or gimmicky styles are hard to read page after page.

If you expect to do a lot of typing in school or during your career, you should give serious thought to buying a typewriter (or word processing printer) with pica type. Pica has larger letters and gives ten characters to the inch. Teachers and editors prefer to read pica over elite, which is smaller, at twelve characters to the inch.

**9.4.4. Margins.** Term papers are double-spaced and have generous margins so that instructors will have room in which to write comments. The margin requirements are:

- Left side and top: Use a margin of one and a half inches.
- Right side and bottom: Use a margin of one inch.

**9.4.5. Numbering the pages.** The page number is placed in the upper right corner of each page, one inch down from the top of the paper and one inch in from the right edge, not from the right margin. The last digit of each number is placed against the margin.

Page 1 is the first page of the introduction, and numbering is consecutive throughout the paper.

You may wish to place your last name on each page just to the left of the page number. This practice helps identify the paper should the pages get mixed up with the work of another student.

**9.4.6. Justified (even) right margins.** Word processing printers can be programmed to provide justified (even) right margins. Check with your instructor before using this feature. Many instructors prefer that term papers be prepared the standard way, with ragged (uneven) right margins.

**9.4.7. End-of-line word divisions.** Avoid dividing a word at the end of a line. Instead, type the line shorter and place the entire word at the start of the next line.

**9.4.8. Indentation.** The following requirements apply to indented items:

- Begin a new paragraph by indenting five spaces from the left margin.
- A block-indented quotation is indented five spaces from the left and right margins.

CROSS-REFERENCE: Indentation is different for endnotes and bibliographies. See section 9.4.18.

**9.4.9. Typing the dash.** The dash (—) is made on a typewriter by striking the hyphen (-) key twice. If you are using word processing equipment that has a special key for the dash, that key should be used.

**9.4.10. Use of underlining.** In a term paper underlining is used to show items that are italicized in published material. An example is the title of a book. The italicized title *Everyone in the Bible* appears in a term paper as this:

```
Everyone in the Bible
```

It is not necessary to underline the spaces between words. A continuous line is easier to type, however, and doing so ensures that the title's punctuation will be underlined.

**9.4.11. Spacing with punctuation.** The following spacing requirements apply to the various punctuation marks:

- After a sentence's ending punctuation leave two spaces.
- After a comma or a semicolon leave one space.
- Before and after a dash or a hyphen leave no space.

- After a colon leave two spaces, except that no spacing is placed on either side of a colon in scriptural references (Ruth 3:2-5), with hours and minutes (10:18 p.m.), and with volume and page number (1:14-17).
- Before an opening (initial) parenthesis or bracket, leave one space. Between the opening parenthesis or bracket and the first letter following, leave no space. Before a closing parenthesis or bracket, leave no space. After a closing parenthesis or bracket, (1) leave no space before any following punctuation, or (2) leave one space before the first letter following.

**9.4.12. Spacing with initials and abbreviations.** Many abbreviations can be written without internal periods. That is, *American Medical Association* can be abbreviated as *AMA*, not *A.M.A.* Otherwise, the spacing requirements for abbreviations of personal and organizational names are:

- Use single spacing between the periods and initials of a person's name (J. B. Brady). In some cases, popular usage has eliminated the spacing and the periods from a person's initials (FDR).
- Use no spacing between the periods and letters of initials of an organization (U.S. Steel), unless the organization uses some other style.

**9.4.13. Title page.** To type the title page, follow these instructions:

- All items on the title page are centered between the left and right edges of the page, not the margins.

- Type the title four inches down from the top of the page.
- Double-space down and type the subtitle if used.

**NOTE 1:** Do not underline the title and subtitle, and do not place them in quotation marks. Use underlining or quotation marks in the title and subtitle the same as you would for words that appear in the text.

**NOTE 2:** To capitalize title and subtitle, follow these instructions: Capitalize the first and last words and all other words except articles (*a, an, the*); prepositions (words such as *to, in, with, through*); and conjunctions (words such as *and, for, but*).

- Drop down two inches and type your name.
- Double-space down and type the school's name.
- Double-space down and type the course name and number.
- Double-space down and type the date the paper will be turned in.

**9.4.14. Table of contents.** If your paper has a table of contents, it is typed after the paper is completed and the pages are numbered.

- Just below the top margin and centered between the left and right margins, place the words *Table of Contents*. Do not use quotation marks around that heading and do not underline it.
- Drop down four spaces. At the left margin type *Contents*, and at the right margin type *Page*. Underline both, but do not place them in quotation marks.

- Drop down four spaces and begin typing headings and page numbers. You may use a row of periods to connect a heading to its page number. Use double-spacing between headings. Headings are taken from the paper and are not placed in quotation marks and are not underlined. If headings are numbered, the numbers are aligned vertically on the periods:

I.
II.
III.

The table of contents is an unnumbered page.

**9.4.15. First page.** The first page of the paper is the page on which your introductory material begins. This page appears immediately after the table of contents, if one is used. If a table of contents is not used, the first page appears immediately after the title page. The typing instructions are:

- Place the paper's title four spaces below the top margin, centered between the left and right margins.
- Double-space down and type the subtitle, if used; the subtitle is centered between the left and right margins.
- Make sure that the title and subtitle are copied exactly from the title page.
- Drop down four lines and type the heading *Introduction*, if you are using headings. If not, begin typing the introduction.

**9.4.16. Text.** The text is typed double-spaced. Some specific provisions are:

- For the typing of quotations, see section 6.2.
- For the typing of headings, see figure 9a.
- For the typing of tables, see section 7.3.

**9.4.17. Endnotes and bibliographies.** Endnotes begin on a separate sheet, as does the bibliography. The headings used are *Notes* and *Bibliography*, at the top of the page and centered between the margins. Do not underline these headings and do not place quotation marks around them. Drop down four spaces from each heading and begin typing, following the requirements of subsections 9.4.18 through 9.4.20.

**9.4.18. Indentation and alignment of endnotes and bibliographies.** Hanging indentation is used with endnotes and bibliographies. That is, the first line of each entry begins at the left margin, and subsequent lines are indented according to these guidelines:

- For a bibliography, place the first letter of each line against the left margin. In the same entry, indent all lines other than the first five spaces from the left margin.
- For a list of notes, place the numeral against the left margin. Place a period after the numeral, leave two blank spaces, and begin typing the first line. Subsequent lines in the same entry are aligned under the first letter of the first line.

When a list of notes contains more than nine items, vertical alignment will have to be made on the periods following note numbers. The largest number is placed against the left margin.

```
  1. ...........................................
 10. ...........................................
101. ...........................................
```

**9.4.19. Vertical spacing.** Endnotes and bibliographies are typed double-spaced throughout, within entries and between entries.

**9.4.20. Horizontal spacing.** Horizontal spacing follows this style:

- After ending punctuation, leave two spaces.
- After a comma or semicolon, leave one space.
- Before and after a dash or a hyphen, leave no space.
- When a colon is used with volume and series or page number, leave no space (2:21-25).
- Before an opening (initial) parenthesis or bracket, leave one space.
- Between the opening parenthesis or bracket and the first character following, leave no space.
- Before a closing parenthesis or bracket, leave no space.
- After a closing parenthesis or bracket, (1) leave no space before any following punctuation, or (2) leave one space before the first character following.

**9.4.21. Making corrections.** Strikeovers are not permitted, and corrections should be limited to two or three per page. That statement holds true whether you erase and retype, use correction fluid, or make changes with a pen. If corrections exceed two or three per page, retype the page.

**9.4.22. Fastening the pages.** Staple or clip the pages together in the upper left-hand corner. *Do not* place the paper in a binder unless your instructor tells you to do so. In addition, do not place a row of staples along the left edge of the pages. When you do that, you make it harder for the instructor to flip the pages.

## 9.5. Proofreading Pointers

You proofread your paper to catch problems such as spelling mistakes or typographical errors. You can improve your proofreading skills by following these steps:

- If you are typing the paper, proofread while the page is in the typewriter. Roll the page so that you proofread one line at a time.
- If you are using a word processor, proofread on the screen and on the printout. A printer malfunction may build in an error that doesn't show on the screen.
- If your word processing system has a spell-checking program, use it, but do not rely on it 100 percent.
- Try to find someone to proofread with. One person reads out loud from the next-to-last version, enunciates clearly, and announces punctuation marks. The other person follows along on the final version.
- When you are proofreading by yourself, begin at the front and proofread *everything* straight through to the end. *Everything* means that you closely and slowly read each *letter* of each word, each *punctuation mark*, and each *number*.

- Read pages backward or out of order. Changing the sequence allows you to view the material from a different perspective.
- Read slowly. If you do not read slowly, you are not proofreading; you are reading.
- If you find one typographical error, look for others nearby. Mistakes tend to cluster.
- Make sure that headings and page numbers match those in the table of contents.
- Double-check all math and calculations. Be alert for misplaced commas and decimal points.
- Make sure that figure and table numbers in the text match those on the figures and tables.
- Carefully check items that appear in sets. These include brackets, dashes, parentheses, and quotation marks.

# APPENDIX

# SAMPLE TERM PAPER

The sample term paper shown here is adapted from one written for a college-level course in American literature. To save space, not all of the paper is presented. Omissions are shown with ellipsis points ( . . . ) or comments placed in square brackets. The paper is typed according to the instructions in section 9.4.

The paper was written to conform to this thesis statement: "This paper will use William Dean Howell's *A Hazard of New Fortunes* and Upton Sinclair's *The Jungle* to show that the urban poor in turn-of-the-century America had little chance for success."

The title page is arranged and typed according to the instructions in section 9.4.13. The term paper's title contains the titles of two books. These two titles are underlined, as is standard. Otherwise, the term paper's title is neither underlined nor placed in quotation marks.

The Urban Poor and the Myth of Success:

As Dramatized in A Hazard of New Fortunes

and The Jungle


Student Name

School Name

Course Name and Number

Date Paper Will Be Turned In


The table of contents is prepared according to the instructions in section 9.4.14.

Table of Contents

The introduction begins on page 1. The title is repeated from the title page, and the heading *Introduction* is used. Instructions for typing the paper's first page are in section 9.4.15.

In the introduction the first paragraph begins by referring to people, and the subject of the paper is not mentioned until the second paragraph. There the language expands upon the wording of the thesis statement. The thesis statement itself is not used in the paper.

The Urban Poor and the Myth of Success:

As Dramatized in A Hazard of New Fortunes

and The Jungle


## INTRODUCTION


In 1860 the average American male was a land-owning yeoman farmer; in 1900 he was an employee. In 1860 the ambitious lad wanted a farm; in 1900 he sought a job. The job was in the city, and people migrated from the American countryside and the meadowlands of Europe to places like New York, Cleveland, and Chicago. The city was a magnet, a challenge of work, and a lure of wealth. Men residing in cities led the world in creating new products and launching vast new industries. With a thousand gleaming lights and a roar of life, the city glamorized hard work, Horatio Algerism, and social Darwinism. Success was in the city.

Not for everyone. One growing class--the urban poor--was not sharing in the American dream. Their plight was dramatized in two turn-of-the-century novels. One is William Dean Howells's A Hazard of New Fortunes. The other is Upton Sinclair's The Jungle. These novels describe tenement life, make statements about social attitudes, and portray the chances of success for the poor in the city.

This paper uses headings as described in section 9.1 and figure 9a.

Some of the quotations used are complete sentences, and others are *fragmentary quotations*. A fragmentary quotation consists of part of a sentence in the original that is worked into a sentence in the paper. Superior numbers, or superscripts, identify the sources of quotations.

The paper makes different uses of combinations of quotation marks. Where you see double quotation marks on the page, no quotation marks appeared in the original. Where you see single marks inside of double in the paper, the original used double marks to show someone talking.

THE RICH, THE POOR, AND THE CITY

The rich in the city. Basil and Isabel March, of A Hazard of New Fortunes, are the rich of the city. Early in the story they are driven on an unplanned trip through a New York slum. The detour reveals little about the poor but a lot about the Marches. The rubbish-strewn street, where a "peddler of cheap fruit urged his cart through the street and mixed his cry with the joyous screams and shouts of the children and the scolding and gossiping voices of the women," where "a drunkard zigzagged down the sidewalk," disgusts Isabel, and she closes her window to the sounds and smells and complains to Basil.[1]

Basil's answer arises from his snobbish,

rationalizing view that the grim simplicity of the
poor life makes it fun, that, despite the
deprivation, the poor adjust to their state
magnificently.  According to him, the poor "'have
to spend their whole lives in it, winter or
summer, with no hopes of driving out of it except
in a hearse.  I must say they don't seem to mind
it.  I haven't seen a jollier crowd anywhere in
New York.'"[2]

   [Three subsequent paragraphs omitted.]

The paper is typed double-spaced throughout. Each
page is numbered in the upper right corner. In the
original the student's name appeared just to the left of
the page number and separated from it by two hyphens.
Like many papers written on literary subjects, this one
was written in the historical present (see section 3.7.3).

   The poor in the city.  One who does not
adjust to the conditions of poverty is Jurgis
Rudkus of Upton Sinclair's The Jungle.  On the
surface, Jurgis is the stereotypical immigrant--
simple, hard working, fun loving, religious, of
peasant stock.  He, his aging father, and ten
soon-to-be in-laws, including six children, leave
Lithuania when one of them suggests they go to
America "where a friend of his had gotten rich."[5]
Jurgis is also the evolutionary immigrant of
social Darwinism.  After his voyage across the

Atlantic he emerges from the water, like the
biological ichthyostega, to walk on land.

Once past the Statue of Liberty, Jurgis goes
into the jungle, not a life-giving green world,
but a harsh reality of concrete and iron where
even the fittest find it hellishly hard to
survive.  Jurgis soon becomes mired in the
ghettos of Chicago and struggles for freedom and
survival against a lengthy, terrifying catalog of
social ills. . . .

Block-indented quotations are typed double-spaced
and indented five spaces from each margin. The identifying superior number appears at the end of the
quotation.

SUFFERING AND SUCCESS

The concept of suffering.  People like Isabel
March say "'I don't believe there's any real
suffering--not real suffering--among those people;
that is, it would be suffering from our point of
view, but they've been used to it all their lives,
and they don't feel the discomfort so much.'"[9]
Jurgis suffers.  The Isabel Marches isolate and
delude themselves and do not realize how much a
Jurgis Rudkus can suffer.  His confidence ebbs, he
feels he is beaten, that life "had thrown him
away."[10]  As Sinclair writes:

He only knew that he was wronged, and
that the world had wronged him; that
the law, that society, with all its
powers, had declared itself his foe.
And every hour his soul grew blacker,
every hour he dreamed new dreams of
vengeance, of defiance, of raging,
frenzied hate.[11]

[Two subsequent paragraphs omitted.]


The formula for success. The apparent
arithmetic for success is ability and
determination plus cleverness (basic intelligence
plus insidious cunning) plus luck. Jurgis has all
the initiative, ambition, and pluck of Horatio
Alger's heroes but he does not have the luck that
the hack writer gave them; there is no rich man's
baby to save from drowning in the bay or snatch
from the burning building. Not only does good
fortune contribute to success, but so does guile,
subtle dishonesty, and "apple polishing."
Although Jurgis can resort to brutal crime in the
streets he cannot face up to and conquer the crude
politics of the stockyards where "if you met a man
who was rising in Packingtown, you met a knave."[16]

[Two subsequent paragraphs omitted.]

Conclusions are called to the reader's attention by the use of headings.

CONCLUSIONS

The test of social Darwinism. Disciples of social Darwinism would point at Jurgis's faults and say "he hasn't met the test. He is obviously not the fittest." Critics of social Darwinism, however, could use Jurgis to prove that survival of the fittest is a falsehood when applied to the human condition. Jurgis is apparently the fittest in The Jungle, demonstrating indefatigable strength and determination, "towering above the rest."[18] If that is the case, his role indicates the absurdity of applying precise biological formulas to abstruse sociological phenomena. . . .

The paper's final paragraph leaves no doubt that the paper has ended.

Poverty and the chances for success. What the Marches are turning their backs to is described in Sinclair's vivid portrait of the sullen face of urban poverty. In what historians call the Modern World, feudal landlords, along with political and industrial bosses, dominate the poor. Proper sanitation and building codes are nonexistent or not enforced. Children play in garbage-filled streets or in the garbage dumps

themselves. . . . For the poor, success is as
remote as a shooting star.

    The final word on any problem in
turn-of-the-century America was always that of
Mr. Dooley, Chicago's shanty-Irish, "Archey-Road"
philosopher:

    "'I'm glad I'm poor,' said Mr. Hennessy.

    "'It gives ye less to talk about but more to
think about,' said Mr. Dooley."[20]

The notes refer to two principal sources. A complete citation is given the first time each source is referred to; shortened forms are used thereafter. In the shortened forms the titles of the books are omitted because the authors' names alone provide enough identification. Titles would have to be mentioned if it was necessary to specify different books by the same author.

### Notes

1.  William Dean Howells, <u>A Hazard of New
    Fortunes</u> (New York:  New American Library,
    1965), 56.

2.  Howells, 57.

3.  Howells, 61.

4.  Howells, 56.

5.  Upton Sinclair, <u>The Jungle</u> (New York:  Lancer
    Books, 1970), 36.

6.  Sinclair, 42.

7.  Sinclair, 42.

8.  Sinclair, 189.

9.  Howells, 60.

10.  Sinclair, 185.

[Notes 11 through 17 deleted.]

18.  Sinclair, 48.

19.  Howells, 61.

20.  Finley Peter Dunne, "Advantages of Poverty,"
     in Observations by Mr. Dooley (New York:
     R. H. Russell, 1902), 146.

# MORE ADVICE ON WRITING

## AN ANNOTATED BIBLIOGRAPHY

### Dictionaries

All of the following are excellent dictionaries.

*American Heritage Dictionary*. 2d college edition. Boston, Massachusetts: Houghton Mifflin Co., 1982. A paperback adaptation is available.

*Random House College Dictionary*. Revised edition. New York: Random House, 1982.

*Webster's Ninth New Collegiate Dictionary*. Springfield, Massachusetts: Merriam-Webster, 1985.

### Research

Brady, John. *The Craft of Interviewing*. New York: Random House, 1977.

A standard work on how to get information out of people.

McCormick, Mona. *The New York Times Guide to Reference Materials*. New York: New American Library, 1986.

A practical paperback guide to finding and using a variety of sources, including computerized data bases.

## Writing

Ehrlich, Eugene. *The Bantam Concise Handbook of English*. New York: Bantam Books, 1986.

Good for a variety of topics including grammar, word usage, and writing in general.

Elbow, Peter. *Writing with Power: Techniques for Mastering the Writing Process*. New York: Oxford University Press, 1981.

Good for some of the hardest aspects of writing: the task of determining audience and the processes of writing and revising. Look elsewhere for specific advice on grammar, style, and word usage.

Follett, Wilson, and others. *Modern American Usage: A Guide*. New York: Hill and Wang, 1966.

*Modern American Usage* was modern when published in 1966 and is still modern today. An excellent book on style and usage.

Kilpatrick, James J. *The Writer's Art*. New York: Andrews, McMeel and Parker, 1984.

Good reading and good advice about grammar, style, and usage.

Zinsser, William Knowlton. *On Writing Well: An Informal Guide to Writing Nonfiction*. Rev. ed. New York: Harper and Row, 1985.

More good advice on writing.

# CHAPTER NOTES

Note numbers identify sources of material used in the text and in the writing samples.

## Chapter 2. Research

1. George Garrett, *The Writer's Voice: Conversations with Contemporary Writers* (New York: William Morrow and Company, 1973), p. 156.
2. "Two Writers Question the Originality of *Roots*," *Publishers Weekly* (May 2, 1977), p. 20.
3. "Haley Settles Plagiarism Suit, Concedes Passages," *Publishers Weekly* (December 25, 1978), p. 22.

## Chapter 3. Style and Clarity

1. Alvin Toffler, *The Third Wave* (New York: Bantam Books, 1980), p. 233.
2. Sebastian de Grazia, *Of Time, Work, and Leisure* (Garden City, New York: Doubleday and Company, Inc., 1962), p. 373.

3. Vance Packard, *The People Shapers* (New York: Bantam Books, 1977), p. 242.

## Chapter 6. Quotations

1. Edward Waldo Emerson and Waldo Emerson Forbes, eds., *Journals of Ralph Waldo Emerson, 1849–1855*, vol. 8 (Boston, Massachusetts: Houghton Mifflin Co., 1912), p. 20.
2. Frank Rose, *Into the Heart of the Mind: An American Quest for Artificial Intelligence* (New York: Harper & Row, 1984), p. 12.
3. *The Epic of Gilgamesh* (Baltimore, Maryland: Penguin Books, 1972), p. 61.
4. Robert Herrick, "To the Virgins, to Make Much of Time," in Oscar Williams, ed., *Master Poems of the English Language* (New York: Washington Square Press, 1966), p. 141.
5. Edward Taylor, "Upon a Spider Catching a Fly," in Oscar Williams and Edwin Honig, eds., *The Mentor Book of Major American Poets* (New York: New American Library, 1962), p. 33.
6. Edgar Allan Poe, "The Raven," in Williams and Honig, *Major American Poets*, p. 105.
7. Samuel Taylor Coleridge, *The Rime of the Ancient Mariner*, in Williams, *Master Poems*, p. 481.
8. Aldo Leopold, *A Sand County Almanac* (New York: Oxford University Press, 1949), p. vii.
9. *Bartlett's Familiar Quotations*, 15th ed., "Donald Francis Mason."
10. *Bartlett's Familiar Quotations*, 15th ed., "Mohandas Karamchand [Mahatma] Gandhi."

11. Rachel L. Carson, *The Sea Around Us,* rev. ed. (New York: Oxford University Press, 1961), p. 209.
12. Margaret Craven, *I Heard the Owl Call My Name* (Garden City, New York: Doubleday and Company, 1973), p. 12.
13. Page Smith, *The Rise of Industrial America* (New York: McGraw-Hill Book Company, 1984), p. 844.
14. Smith, *Industrial America,* p. 841.
15. Thomas Carew, "Song," in Williams, *Master Poems,* p. 153.
16. Gail Sheehy, *Passages: Predictable Crises of Adult Life* (New York: E. P. Dutton and Company, 1974), p. 129.
17. Daniel J. Boorstin, *The Discoverers* (New York: Random House, 1983), p. 296.

## Chapter 7. Graphics

1. *Statistical Abstract of the United States* (Washington, D.C.; U.S. Government Printing Office, 1986), p. 151.
2. Sidney S. Culbert, "The Principal Languages of the World," in *The World Almanac and Book of Facts* (New York: Newspaper Enterprise Association, 1985), p. 245.
3. U.S. Bureau of the Census, *World Almanac,* p. 252.
4. News Election Service, "Presidential Elections," *World Almanac,* p. 40.
5. *Statistical Abstract of the United States,* p. 151.
6. *Statistical Abstract of the United States,* p. 151.

# INDEX